MW01492557

My Steps, My Stumbles, and My Stops
Are Ordered by the Lord

VOLUME I
VICTORY OVER REJECTION

MAE BELL HARRISON AND LORI SANDERS

Halo
PUBLISHING
INTERNATIONAL

ISBN: 978-1-63765-206-0
LCCN: 2022904103

Halo Publishing International, LLC
www.halopublishing.com

Printed and bound in the United States of America

Mae Bell

I would like to dedicate this book to my Lord and Savior Jesus Christ Who has been with me for eighty-eight years. I know that I've only come this far because of His love for me, His daughter. I can't thank Him enough for the many blessings, including this memoir revealing a snapshot of my life for my children and generations to see.

Also, I dedicate this book to my children and grandchildren. Words can't express my love and gratitude for you all. You all have been by my side, not just in the good times, but when it was rough. There are moments that we shared laughter, heartache, pain, celebrations, and disagreements, but please know that although my love is given to each of you differently, it is an EQUAL LOVE. You ALL have made me laugh, and you all have made me cry, but I pray for each and every one of you daily, calling all fifty-three of you by name. As you become parents and grandparents, I pray you understand the answers to your "Mom, why?"

I love you all so much and pray that God will bless you indeed. Walk in your God-given assignments. You're never too old—I have become an author at eighty-eight.

"But seek first His kingdom and his righteousness, and ALL these things will be given to you as well" (Matthew 6:33, New International Version).

Lori

I would like to thank my Heavenly Father Jesus, Who is the true author and finisher of my faith. Lord, I thank You for giving me the vision in 2012. You said, "Write the vision and make it plain so that my children and grandchildren may run to it" (Habakkuk 2:2, paraphrased). Lord, I pray that millions will be blessed, but especially my children and grandchildren on a deeper level.

Thank you to my queen, my number one spiritual mentor, my shero, my mom for allowing me to help write your story. I love you so much! You're the best mom that I could have asked for. You have shown your love, grace and mercy toward me when I didn't deserve it.

Thank you to my boo/hubby, Nevin Sanders, for your patience and the countless days you sacrificed your time to allow me to go up in the office and write my mom's story. You will always be my king. I love you unconditionally. You have pushed this insecure girl since the age of twenty-one to know my worth. Every achievement that God has blessed me with has your name in the equation. I love you, BOO!

Thank you to my son, Lionel Harrison, you are the BEST SON a mom could pray for. You spoil me and make me feel an undeserved and unconditional love from you. I know I was hard on you as a young parent because I simply wanted you to soar. You have done that and more. Thank you for your hand in this book. The value of your illustrations and your assistance in marketing this book is beyond words. Continue to make me proud, and keep God as the foundation of anything you touch. I love you so much!

Thank you to my daughter-in-love, Javonda Harrison; you are the daughter-in-law for whom I prayed for my son when he was only eight years old. Thank you for all you do! I appreciate your coaching me, editing my work, creating the About the Book, and contributing to this project in so many ways vital to our finishing it. I love you and am grateful that you love my son unconditionally.

Thank you to my grandchildren!

Ayanna Harrison, you changed my name from Nana to Nanny. You will always be my princess. I will forever love you unconditionally and pray that you will thrive as you walk in your purpose. You are gifted and possess the talent of a creative imagination. May God bless your gift, and may you use it to His glory. I remember we started writing our books around the same time. I can't wait to see yours get published.

Logan Harrison, you are my handsome Loggie Bear. You are my logical thinker. You are a mini-me version of your father. I pray blessings over your future. Keep God first so that whatever you touch will multiply with blessings. Please know that you are fearfully and wonderfully made.

Leia Harrison, you are our li'l diva; we have no clue where you got that, but be you. We love it! You are creative as well. We know that God has so much in store for you if you simply stay close to Him. Whatever you do, seek God for guidance and wisdom.

To my bonus family, Nevin's sons and grandchildren: Brian, Eric, Jessie, Jonathan. and Ora. May God bless you all and your future families. I love you all dearly! Thank you for allowing me to be a part of the Sanders clan for these few decades.

To my two remaining siblings, Sadie and Freda, I will love you all forever. Thanks for allowing me to be your little sister. You two have been blessings in my life. I praise God for restoring our closeness when the enemy thought he had us. Love you, Sadie! Yes, you have always been the family's princess. Love you, Freda! Yes, you are the mini version of Mom; many, if not all, family members feel comfortable going to you as a confidante.

To my nieces and nephews, keep pushing for your calling in life. DON'T QUIT! DON'T GIVE UP! STAY FOCUSED! Love you all and your children: Darcel, Richard, Tony, Tina, Sharene, Evalena, Cortez, April, Daylen, Theresa, Martin, Tyrone, Tamara, and Faith!

To all my extended family and friends who prayed for me and this project, thank you! I can't name them all, but to Kim Peterson and Sherry Williams, I must give a special shout-out for the years of this being on our prayer list. Thank you, ladies, for your unconditional love through good and tough times; we will forever be sisters. Thank you to Tammy Gaffney and Thomas Locke for your input as authors. Thank you to all my friends who reviewed the cover options and gave their honest input. I love you all.

Thank you to Pastor Kevin James and Sis Tanya James of New Community Bible Fellowship for having the best church for me in the Greater Cleveland, Ohio, area. Thank you for being the best spiritual parents for me in this season. Love you much!

A big thank-you to Halo Publishing for making the dream of my mom's memoir become a reality.

A big thank-you to Matt Kirksey for your amazing photography work. You got Mom and me looking cute as new authors. Appreciate you, bro!

Thank you, Alisa Tyler, for your assistance on photo day and your referrals to help complete this project. I truly love and appreciate you.

Contents

INTRODUCTION

Mae Bell Young Harrison: Her Story

The LORD makes firm the steps of the one who delights in Him; though he may stumble, he will not fall, for the LORD upholds him with His hand (Psalms 37:23–24).

The title of this book, *My Steps, My Stumbles, and My Stops Are Ordered by the Lord,* and the use of Scripture, Psalms 37:23–24, were influenced by a paper I wrote twenty-five-plus years ago; it was submitted to my former church for use as one of the church's weekly articles. Although the paper was not used as an article, I kept it close to me because God used that paper to get me through life's challenges.

Initially, I felt rejected that my writing was not accepted, but God had a reason. Over the years, I have learned that nothing can happen in my life without God's permission. Now, my daughter and I are putting my steps, my stumbles, and my stops in the pages of this book. Come take this journey with me to witness God in the midst of ALL my trials and triumphs.

As I grew spiritually over the years, and continue to grow, I look back and see how the Lord has brought me through "stuff" and allowed me to sustain during tough times. Later in the book, I will share a stop in my life when my husband had *kidney disease/renal failure. He had to have dialysis three times per week, causing him to resign from his job as an auto-body painter and our household earnings to be reduced to only Social Security Disability Income monthly payments.*

Through the storms of life, I give God praise that even after the passing of my husband, who survived seven years on dialysis, my family and I pulled through. Although income was scarce, and the struggle was real, we were never to the point of losing our home. As a single mom of teenagers and young adults, none of my children was ever incarcerated or pulled into this world addicted to drugs or alcoholism. When I look back thirty years, forty years, fifty years, and sixty years later, I see that my steps were ordered by God. "He alone knows my down setting and uprising and is acquainted with all my ways" (Psalms 139:3, paraphrased).

I am eighty-eight and can say, even having been through life's challenges, I'm blessed and highly favored! I pray these pages will touch your life and encourage you to know that whatever life challenges you face, God knows your situation and has entrusted you with a personal assignment to bring glory to His name.

I hope you enjoy the journey of *My Steps, My Stumbles, and My Stops Are Ordered by the Lord, Volume I!*

CHAPTER 1

The Man with the "Pretty" Legs

Meet the Parents: The Young Man with the Short Pants and "Pretty" Legs

There he was, standing across the room, allowing his chocolate, attractive, fine legs with strong calves to be highly visible in his short pants. Wearing short pants at church was not uncommon for a young man of his age, but his attire gave Sadie an innocent pleasure to behold. She gave a chuckle and with humor asked, "Who is the man with those pretty legs?"

Fletcher with the "pretty" legs was equally observing of Sadie's beauty.

These are my parents, Fletcher and Sadie Mae, who noticed one another at Mount Pleasant Baptist Church, also known as Mount Plez, in the red hills of Meridian, Mississippi. Although my father was a member of Oak Tivvey Baptist Church, also known as Oak Tiv, both churches would periodically fellowship together for afternoon services.

After numerous occasions of church fellowships and observing one another, someone finally introduced them during one of the afternoon services. They decided to date, and the rest was history. They exchanged their nuptials during the summer of 1927.

As a young couple with little resources, they resided with my father's parents, Mose and Alice. Also, my mother made the sacrifice to follow the spiritual leadership of her husband and left Mount Plez, worshipping thereafter with him at Oak Tiv.

My paternal grandparents were terrific people, but their lifestyle was different to what my mother was accustomed. It was told that my mother lost a great deal of weight because an abundance of food was not provided in her in-laws' home. Although Grandpa Mose was a godly, hardworking man, he was a private man full of pride. During a challenging financial season in his life when my mom resided with them, he would not reach out for help. It was a no-no to him to borrow from other people. He would go hungry before asking for handouts.

One Sunday, Mount Pleasant, my mother's old church, was having a Homecoming service, a special service to which all the alumni—past members of the church who have moved away or are worshipping at a different church—are invited for worship, fellowship, and sharing a meal. If you are familiar with Southern churches, Homecoming Sunday's dinner includes, but is not limited to, a bounty of Southern-fried chicken, collard greens, black-eyed peas, macaroni and cheese, and homemade dinner rolls; for dessert, homemade pies, cakes, butter rolls, and cobblers overflowing.

My mother attended; being close to the due date of her first child, she ate and thoroughly enjoyed the abundance of food. Later that evening, after taking pleasure in the Homecoming, she told my father in a respectful manner that she was not going back to Oak Tivvey and would no longer reside far from her biological family. She said, "We are going to have to find a place close to Mount Pleasant."

Shortly after that conversation, they moved in with her parents, Daniel Rufus and Blandenia Moore, for one week until my father, being the hard worker he was, found a home for less than four dollars per month for rent. They moved into their home exactly six months after their marriage.

Oh, the joy that filled my mother's soul at residing near her childhood church and, more importantly, close to her parents and siblings, who would form the support team for their firstborn child. Mom had high regards and love for my father's parents, despite Grandpa Mose's pride, but she was elated to be around her mother and siblings, to whom she was remarkably close.

As time progressed, God blessed Grandpa Mose; his latter days were greater than his hardship season. Grandpa Mose was able to acquire two homes and multiple acres of land.

The Nervous Breakdown

My mother was ecstatic to be back on her side of town because she treasured sibling love. Also, she valued the importance of being a godly wife, which included being a helpmate to my father. Although Mom and Dad both had strong personalities and leadership skills that drove them to take charge and make things happen, they had a respect and love that supported one another's ideas and goals, naturally working as a team. They had a great team dynamic, especially when it came to their work ethics. They both took pride in building a farm a few acres at a time. Over the years, they grew their farm to produce acres of various beans, peas, corn, tomatoes, watermelons, cotton, and livestock, which included goats, chickens, cows, hogs, pigs, and horses. Dad provided for his family by using the various resources from his land. He grew and sold vegetables to support his family, but also sold kindling from the land. *Kindling* is a term used for the small sticks and twigs that are easily combustible and used for starting fires. Kindling was used in the wood-burning stoves designed for cooking. Although gas cookstoves were introduced in the early 1900s, they were not iconic in many of the Southern Black homes.

Dad was not a man who would sit back in despair because of the Great Depression, no matter how it affected his current situation. He used what was in his hands, his acres of land. This season of my parents' lives reminds me of Exodus 4:2 when the Lord challenged Moses and said, "What is that in your hand?" Do not be troubled by your situation, but trust God and use the resources that He has given you in this season.

It was not long after their move that Dad and Mom had their oldest son, Robert, in April 1928. The following year my sister, Fannie Mae, was born in June 1929, and the year after that my youngest brother, Mozell, was born in December 1930.

Shortly after that, something strange happened; my mom began to regressed to playing with dolls. She acted as if she were a little girl. The responsibility of raising three small children possibly took a toll on her that caused her to have a nervous breakdown. Other family members may argue that a woman who was attracted to my father had "thrown at"—used what we call voodoo powers and put a curse on—my mother and caused the nervous breakdown. Nevertheless, my mom was no longer the strong woman whom my dad first met. Something happened that changed her mental health state.

During my mom's period of mental illness, my father and grandmother thought it would be best for my parents and three siblings to move back with my maternal grandmother so that, while my father was working, she could help take care of my mother and my siblings.

Gramma Blandenia had a huge home in which, for a small rental fee, she provided accommodations for multiple families. Her house had a great big wide, long hallway with rooms on both sides. The living room was called the front room; there was a spacious kitchen and a huge dining room that allowed all the families to be able to sit and dine comfortably. Also, her home had a front and back porches.

As mentioned, my mother reverted to acting like a little girl; she made mud pies and played with dolls and tea sets. For fourteen months, she was not aware that she was a wife and mother. The doctor told Grandma Blandenia that the only way my mother, her daughter, would survive the breakdown was for her to become pregnant again. Regardless that Mom did not recognize her three little children or her husband and she'd gravitated toward dolls, which the doctor saw as an indication of nurturing, the doctor assumed that another baby, despite adding to the responsibility of the other three, would cause her to be healed.

In 1933, she became pregnant. During this time, my maternal grandmother read Psalms 119:1–176 to my mother three times a day. Yes, the longest chapter in the Bible. After a time, she was finally able to get my mother to read it repeatedly.

In June 1934, I was born. Mabel they called me, short for Mae Bell. Although my mom was healing and seemingly somewhat back to normal, my mother could not bond with me, and it seemed that her love for my father was never the same after the nervous breakdown. Although she talked about how much she loved my father, and in her own way sup-ported my dad, her actions and behavior were different. My mother had questions that needed to be answered—such as, how did I get pregnant? when did this happen? why didn't I have a say? who gave "you," her husband, permission to do this to me without my consent? and what else happened during those fourteen months that I was incapacitated?

There were many questions that took years for my mother to address and process. Although the newborn was a blessing, and the delivery brought her out of the nervous breakdown, she tended to focus on the pain of the various questions that were unsettling her mind. Over the years, as my mother rested more in the Lord, her faith was restored and strength-ened, and she became the mother and wife needed for the family to survive.

We stayed with Gramma Blandenia for a while after I was born. At six weeks old, the enemy attacked my family again. I had clusters of risens, boils, in my eyes, nose, and ears, making my face looking disfigured. The country doctor said because of my young age, I would not survive the risens. Although the remote general practitioner tried to treat the boils, they became worse. The doctor was faithful in making house visits to check on me. He would come around once a week. He and my family were praying for a miracle healing.

He said, if I lived, no one would want to look at me if I stayed in that condition.

During that time, my aunt was providing lodging for three sanctified preachers in her home; they were aware of my condition and asked my mom if they could pray over me. The three preachers prayed, rebuking Satan and saying how cruel it was to attack a small child.

Later, everyone went to sleep, and my mom came to check in on me. She saw that I was covered in what some would call corruption; the risens had burst, and pus was covering my face. Mom thought I had died of suffocation from the drainage all over my face. She screamed, waking up the entire house.

They all gathered and cried. It was all my mom's siblings and their families, including Uncle Luther and his family, Uncle Willie and his family, Uncle Johnnie, Aunt Mary Ella, Dad, and my siblings. After hearing all the crying and commotion, it was told that I began crying.

Gramma Blandenia came and held me, cleaned me up, and told everyone in the house to hush. She said, "Cut out that noise! She's alive."

Immediately, my eyes went back into place. The family rejoiced! For years, the risens left me with a defect that when I ate, food would come out of my nose. This small matter caused isolation. Many of my cousins and some siblings didn't want to be around me when I ate; they thought it was embarrassing.

You're blessed when you stay on course,

walking steadily on the road revealed by GOD.

You're blessed when you follow his directions,

doing your best to find him.

That is right—you don't go off on your own;

you walk straight along the road he set.

You, GOD, prescribed the right way to live;

now you expect us to live it.

Oh, that my steps might be steady,

keeping to the course you set;

Then I'd never have any regrets

in comparing my life with your counsel.

I thank you for speaking straight from your heart;

I learn the pattern of your righteous ways.

I'm going to do what you tell me to do;

don't ever walk off and leave me.

***

How can a young person live a clean life?

By carefully reading the map of your Word.

I'm single-minded in pursuit of you;

don't let me miss the road signs you've posted.

I've banked your promises in the vault of my heart

so I won't sin myself bankrupt.

Be blessed, GOD;

train me in your ways of wise living.

I'll transfer to my lips

all the counsel that comes from your mouth;
I delight far more in what you tell me about living
than in gathering a pile of riches.
I ponder every morsel of wisdom from you;
I attentively watch how you've done it.
I relish everything you've told me of life,
I won't forget a word of it.

Be generous with me and I'll live a full life;
not for a minute will I take my eyes off your road.
Open my eyes so I can see
what you show me of your miracle-wonders.
I'm a stranger in these parts;
give me clear directions.
My soul is starved and hungry, ravenous!—
insatiable for your nourishing commands.
And those who think they know so much,
ignoring everything you tell them—let them have it!
Don't let them mock and humiliate me;
I've been careful to do just what you said.
While bad neighbors maliciously gossip about me,
I'm absorbed in pondering your wise counsel.
Yes, your sayings on life are what give me delight;
I listen to them as to good neighbors!

I'm feeling terrible—I couldn't feel worse!
Get me on my feet again. You promised, remember?

When I told my story, you responded;
train me well in your deep wisdom.
Help me understand these things inside and out
so I can ponder your miracle-wonders.
My sad life's dilapidated, a falling-down barn;
build me up again by your Word.
Barricade the road that goes nowhere;
grace me with your clear revelation.
I choose the true road to somewhere;
I post your road signs at every curve and corner.
I grasp and cling to whatever you tell me;
GOD, don't let me down!
I'll run the course you lay out for me
if you'll just show me how.

GOD, teach me lessons for living
so I can stay the course.
Give me insight so I can do what you tell me—
my whole life one long, obedient response.
Guide me down the road of your commandments;
I love traveling this freeway!
Give me a bent for your words of wisdom,
and not for piling up loot.
Divert my eyes from toys and trinkets,
invigorate me on the pilgrim way.
Affirm your promises to me—
promises made to all who fear you.

Deflect the harsh words of my critics—
but what you say is always so good.
See how hungry I am for your counsel;
preserve my life through your righteous ways!

*Let your love, G*OD*, shape my life*
with salvation, exactly as you promised;
Then I'll be able to stand up to mockery
because I trusted your Word.
Don't ever deprive me of truth, not ever—
your commandments are what I depend on.
Oh, I'll guard with my life what you've revealed to me,
guard it now, guard it ever;
And I'll stride freely through wide open spaces
as I look for your truth and your wisdom;
Then I'll tell the world what I find,
speak out boldly in public, unembarrassed.
I cherish your commandments—oh, how I love them!—
relishing every fragment of your counsel.

Remember what you said to me, your servant—
I hang on to these words for dear life!
These words hold me up in bad times;
yes, your promises rejuvenate me.
The insolent ridicule me without mercy,
but I don't budge from your revelation.
I watch for your ancient landmark words,

and know I'm on the right track.
But when I see the wicked ignore your directions,
I'm beside myself with anger.
I set your instructions to music
and sing them as I walk this pilgrim way.
I meditate on your name all night, GOD,
treasuring your revelation, O GOD.
Still, I walk through a rain of derision
because I live by your Word and counsel.

Because you have satisfied me, GOD, I promise
to do everything you say.
I beg you from the bottom of my heart: smile,
be gracious to me just as you promised.
When I took a long, careful look at your ways,
I got my feet back on the trail you blazed.
I was up at once, didn't drag my feet,
was quick to follow your orders.
The wicked hemmed me in—there was no way out—
but not for a minute did I forget your plan for me.
I get up in the middle of the night to thank you;
your decisions are so right, so true—I can't wait till morning!
I'm a friend and companion of all who fear you,
of those committed to living by your rules.
Your love, GOD, fills the earth!
Train me to live by your counsel.

*Be good to your servant, G*OD*;*
　be as good as your Word.
Train me in good common sense;
I'm thoroughly committed to living your way.
Before I learned to answer you, I wandered all over the place,
but now I'm in step with your Word.
You are good, and the source of good;
train me in your goodness.
The godless spread lies about me,
but I focus my attention on what you are saying;
They're bland as a bucket of lard,
while I dance to the tune of your revelation.
My troubles turned out all for the best —
they forced me to learn from your textbook.
Truth from your mouth means more to me
than striking it rich in a gold mine.

With your very own hands you formed me;
now breathe your wisdom over me so I can understand you.
When they see me waiting, expecting your Word,
those who fear you will take heart and be glad.
*I can see now, G*OD*, that your decisions are right;*
your testing has taught me what's true and right.
Oh, love me — and right now! — hold me tight!
just the way you promised.
Now comfort me so I can live, really live;
your revelation is the tune I dance to.

Let the fast-talking tricksters be exposed as frauds;
they tried to sell me a bill of goods,
but I kept my mind fixed on your counsel.
Let those who fear you turn to me
for evidence of your wise guidance.
And let me live whole and holy, soul and body,
so I can always walk with my head held high.

I'm homesick—longing for your salvation;
I'm waiting for your word of hope.
My eyes grow heavy watching for some sign of your promise;
how long must I wait for your comfort?
There's smoke in my eyes—they burn and water,
but I keep a steady gaze on the instructions you post.
How long do I have to put up with all this?
How long till you haul my tormentors into court?
The arrogant godless try to throw me off track,
ignorant as they are of God and his ways.
Everything you command is a sure thing,
but they harass me with lies. Help!
They've pushed and pushed—they never let up—
but I haven't relaxed my grip on your counsel.
In your great love revive me
so I can alertly obey your every word.

What you say goes, GOD,
and stays, as permanent as the heavens.
Your truth never goes out of fashion;
it's as up-to-date as the earth when the sun comes up.

Your Word and truth are dependable as ever;
that's what you ordered—you set the earth going.
If your revelation hadn't delighted me so,
I would have given up when the hard times came.
But I'll never forget the advice you gave me;
you saved my life with those wise words.
Save me! I'm all yours.
I look high and low for your words of wisdom.
The wicked lie in ambush to destroy me,
but I'm only concerned with your plans for me.
I see the limits to everything human,
but the horizons can't contain your commands!

Oh, how I love all you've revealed;
I reverently ponder it all the day long.
Your commands give me an edge on my enemies;
they never become obsolete.
I've even become smarter than my teachers
since I've pondered and absorbed your counsel.
I've become wiser than the wise old sages
simply by doing what you tell me.
I watch my step, avoiding the ditches and ruts of evil
so I can spend all my time keeping your Word.
I never make detours from the route you laid out;
you gave me such good directions.
Your words are so choice, so tasty;
I prefer them to the best home cooking.
With your instruction, I understand life;
that's why I hate false propaganda.

By your words I can see where I'm going;
they throw a beam of light on my dark path.
I've committed myself and I'll never turn back
from living by your righteous order.
Everything's falling apart on me, GOD;
put me together again with your Word.
Festoon me with your finest sayings, GOD;
teach me your holy rules.
My life is as close as my own hands,
but I don't forget what you have revealed.
The wicked do their best to throw me off track,
but I don't swerve an inch from your course.
I inherited your book on living; it's mine forever—
what a gift! And how happy it makes me!
I concentrate on doing exactly what you say—
I always have and always will.

I hate the two-faced, but I love your clear-cut revelation.
You're my place of quiet retreat;
I wait for your Word to renew me.
Get out of my life, evildoers,
so I can keep my God's commands.
Take my side as you promised; I'll live then for sure.
Don't disappoint all my grand hopes.
Stick with me and I'll be all right;
I'll give total allegiance to your definitions of life.
Expose all who drift away from your sayings;

their casual idolatry is lethal.
You reject earth's wicked as so much rubbish;
therefore I lovingly embrace everything you say.
I shiver in awe before you;
your decisions leave me speechless with reverence.

I stood up for justice and the right;
don't leave me to the mercy of my oppressors.
Take the side of your servant, good God;
don't let the godless take advantage of me.
I can't keep my eyes open any longer,
waiting for you to keep your promise to set everything right.
Let your love dictate how you deal with me;
teach me from your textbook on life.
I'm your servant—help me understand what that means,
the inner meaning of your instructions.
It's time to act, GOD;
they've made a shambles of your revelation!
Yea-Saying God, I love what you command,
I love it better than gold and gemstones;
Yea-Saying God, I honor everything you tell me,
I despise every deceitful detour.

Every word you give me is a miracle word—
how could I help but obe
Break open your words, let the light shine out,
let ordinary people see the meaning.

Mouth open and panting,
I wanted your commands more than anything.
Turn my way; look kindly on me,
as you always do to those who personally love you.
Steady my steps with your Word of promise
so nothing malign gets the better of me.
Rescue me from the grip of bad men and women
so I can live life your way.
Smile on me, your servant;
teach me the right way to live.
I cry rivers of tears
because nobody's living by your book!

You are right and you do right, GOD;
your decisions are right on target.
You rightly instruct us in how to live
ever faithful to you.
My rivals nearly did me in,
they persistently ignored your commandments.
Your promise has been tested through and through,
and I, your servant, love it dearly.
I'm too young to be important,
but I don't forget what you tell me.
Your righteousness is eternally right,
your revelation is the only truth.
Even though troubles came down on me hard,
your commands always gave me delight.

The way you tell me to live is always right;
help me understand it so I can live to the fullest.

I call out at the top of my lungs,
"GOD! Answer! I'll do whatever you say."
I called to you, "Save me
so I can carry out all your instructions."
I was up before sunrise,
crying for help, hoping for a word from you.
I stayed awake all night,
prayerfully pondering your promise.
In your love, listen to me;
in your justice, GOD, keep me alive.
As those out to get me come closer and closer,
they go farther and farther from the truth you reveal;
But you're the closest of all to me, GOD,
and all your judgments true.
I've known all along from the evidence of your words
that you meant them to last forever.

Take a good look at my trouble, and help me—
I haven't forgotten your revelation.
Take my side and get me out of this;
give me back my life, just as you promised.
"Salvation" is only gibberish to the wicked
because they've never looked it up in your dictionary.
Your mercies, GOD, run into the billions;

following your guidelines, revive me.

My antagonists are too many to count,

but I don't swerve from the directions you gave.

I took one look at the quitters and was filled with loathing;

they walked away from your promises so casually!

Take note of how I love what you tell me;

out of your life of love, prolong my life.

Your words all add up to the sum total:

Truth. Your righteous decisions are eternal.

I've been slandered unmercifully by the politicians,

but my awe at your words keeps me stable.

I'm ecstatic over what you say,

like one who strikes it rich.

I hate lies—can't stand them!—

but I love what you have revealed.

Seven times each day I stop and shout praises

for the way you keep everything running right.

For those who love what you reveal, everything fits—

no stumbling around in the dark for them.

I wait expectantly for your salvation;

GOD, I do what you tell me.

My soul guards and keeps all your instructions—

oh, how much I love them!

I follow your directions, abide by your counsel;

my life's an open book before you.

Let my cry come right into your presence, GOD;
provide me with the insight that comes only from your Word.
Give my request your personal attention;
rescue me on the terms of your promise.
Let praise cascade off my lips;
after all, you've taught me the truth about life!
And let your promises ring from my tongue;
every order you've given is right.
Put your hand out and steady me
since I've chosen to live by your counsel.
I'm homesick, GOD, for your salvation;
I love it when you show yourself!
Invigorate my soul so I can praise you well,
use your decrees to put iron in my soul.
And should I wander off like a lost sheep—seek me!
I'll recognize the sound of your voice.

(Psalm 119:1–176, The Message Version)

Chapter 2

Dear Old Golden School Days

The Three-and-a-Half-Mile Walk to School

In the country, school season was different than the city's normal nine-month school year. The country's school year was from October through February; these months were when it was too cold for planting or harvesting, which means gathering crops. Most homes in the country had farms with livestock and vegetation. Planting on the multiple acres of land was in March and required the hands of all family members. August and September were the months to gather the crops for canning—cooking them and storing them in some sort of jar or can, hence the name.

My mom canned not only vegetables but meat, such as beef. Everything was organic during those times. Livestock roamed freely upon acres of land. Crops grew naturally with no pesticides.

During a school night, the rain came down; I anticipated the long three-and-a-half-mile, wintry walk to the country school that next morning. No matter the weather, like a mail carrier, we walked three and half miles to school in rain or sleet, cold or warm climate. Although we lived in the South, we experienced cold days from time to time. The rain would freeze on the red clay. Walking on the ultisol, red clay, of Mississippi, there was a loud, uncomfortable crack with every step. On cold days, we wore croker sacks—a bag made of burlap or similar material that would hold many pounds of potatoes—to cover our socks and feet and provide support and traction to prevent sliding on the ice.

The country school that I attended was Mount Pleasant, located at the Mount Pleasant Church. All country schools were one-room classrooms at the various country churches. For example, Pleasant Valley School was at Pleasant Valley Church, and Oak Tiv Elementary was located at Oak Tivvey Church.

Lord, Help Me to Learn My Times Table

Mount Pleasant Elementary consisted of one teacher who taught first through eighth grades in one room. She was my cousin, who some said only had an eighth-grade education. She was firm and, as with all educators in those days, believed in corporal punishment, which is physical punishment, such as spanking, paddling, or caning.

Each student would be asked to stand and recite the times table. If you said them incorrectly, you would get hit on the hand with a switch. I recall, when I was in the third grade, missing several of my multiplications of twos. The teacher whipped my hand red. Oh, the pain from her beating my hand with the three long, flexible pieces of wood intertwined that we called a hand switch. As I walked home from school that day, I said, "Lord, help me learn my times table!" I prayed with sincerity and a determination to learn my multiplications, or as we called the, the times tables.

As I entered my house, my mom had me exit immediately to run an errand for her. She had me go to my grandmother's home to pick up a package. En route, I noticed this silver-leaf lard paper located near the mailbox. In case you are wondering, silver leaf is very thin foil, and it is what lard was wrapped in. Lard was not purchased in cans, but in a four-pound pack of silver-leaf lard paper. I picked up the paper, and there on it was the times table that I needed to learn. God had answered my prayers! I went over to my grandmother's as instructed and returned home with excitement.

"Mom! Mom! I know my times table!" I gave my mother the silver-leaf lard paper. My mother noticed the blank paper, but dared not say anything as I stood before her telling her the multiplications of twos. As I completed them, she smiled and seemed so proud of me, but she still did not say anything.

I could not wait to get to school to say my times table. With confidence and standing tall on the inside, no matter how short I was as a third grader, I recited my memorized times table without any mistakes. When I got home that day, I told my mother how well I did in saying my times table "by heart," or as now we say, "by memorization."

My mom graciously said, "Mabel, it was nothing on that lard paper."

I knew then it was God; He used the silver-leaf lard paper to give me the determination to learn my math and avoid the whippings from the teacher. After that, I became one of the smartest students and was at the top of my class.

Mae's Rules

As time passed at Mount Pleasant Elementary, my mother wanted a better education for her children. My fifth-grade school year, she transferred me to a Catholic school. The Catholic schools were "in town," the city, and tuition was affordable for my parents. No longer would I attend the country school where most of the students were family and close friends.

The country culture was indeed a community. Everyone knew one another from the neighborhood or church. The three churches interacted and visited one another for special afternoon services. Attending the Catholic school would take me out of my comfort zone, but, praise God, at least there would be no more three-and-a-half-mile walks to school. My father had a truck, and we commuted to the city.

Although the private school was Catholic, as with any school, it had bullies. Because my tolerance for bullies was zero to none, my stint in Catholic school was noticeably short. Let's just say I did not complete my fifth-grade year. There was a student bully who did not respect Mae's (Mabel's) Rules, as I call them. If you want to be my friend, you must obey Mae's Rules, which are: DO NOT tell me I have a flat nose, I am fat, or my hair is nappy.

One of Mom's employers—my mother cleaned their home and pressed their clothes—gave her a crinkled housecoat. Mom cut it up and sewed it into a dress to fit me since I was short and fat. Oh, how I loved that dress! I wore it with pride, but a bully said something about my dress. Once that student got the attention of others and they laughed, someone started talking about my hair. Although my hair was short, I was angry that they would make comments, such as it was nappy or had not been combed in months. How could they talk about my hair when my mom would comb, brush, oil, and style my hair every morning before school?

Children can be cruel. I wore my feelings on my sleeves and was always ready to fight to cease the teasing. I didn't get along with the students, so my mother transferred me to complete fifth grade at Meridian Baptist Seminary.

I attended and completed the rest of my fifth-grade year at Meridian Baptist Seminary in 1946. I did well academically, but I had a chip on my shoulder. I was "you won't run nothing by me" Mabel. I was waiting for a person to pick on me; I did not mind fighting.

One day, two boys said something that broke one of Mae's Rules, and they suffered the consequences. The only thing I remember is that I snatched both of them, and somehow we all went out the school window and rolled down the embankment on 116th Street in Meridian, Mississippi. Those boys were whupped from the feet up; shirts were torn. I was just dirty. I got up and brushed myself off.

The principal came and got us and yelled, "What is wrong with you?"

Evidently, those boys said something that triggered me to brawl. I never bothered anyone, but if you said anything about my looks, I was ready to tussle. As my mom always said, I wore my feelings on my sleeve. My school days were always rough for me. I thought my only weapon was to fight my way through.

One year, the city reviewed the country schools and concluded that there were not enough pupils in each building, so they decided to consolidate all three schools. They named the new school Taylor Elementary, used the Mount Pleasant location, and bused the children from the Pleasant Valley and Oak Tiv districts. Of course, this was in the late 1940s; therefore, busing was not to desegregate, but simply to have all three African American schools be consolidated into Taylor Elementary in an effort to reduce cost. Desegregation had not yet been defined at that time, especially in schools. Desegregation in schools wasn't required until 1954's Brown versus the Board of Education of Topeka, Kansas.

Private school did not work for me. I was a smart student, but if anyone said anything negative, a fight began. I returned to the country school to complete sixth grade at Taylor Elementary, which had two teachers. One teacher educated the first through third graders, and the other teacher taught the fourth through six grades. No longer were seventh and eighth graders at the same location as the young people.

I completed sixth grade as the valedictorian and delivered the closing or farewell statement at the graduation ceremony.

Oh, You Gonna Change My Grade

Unfortunately, I had to return to Meridian Baptist Seminary to complete seventh through twelfth grades. My mom came up to the school so many times. The last incident was my tenth-grade year. A cute young girl named Geneva, who dressed very nicely, flounced around the classroom, seemingly to be noticed. She hardly ever did her classwork. On a project that I put a great deal of effort into, I only received a C–, but Geneva received a B+.

I was furious because I had worked so hard and put so much time into completing that assignment. I went to the library and health center to do my research and gather all the material needed for my report. My book that I created was thick and tied with three strings because I had so many written pages and pictures that I'd glued on sheets to present a quality report.

I reached over the desk, collared the teacher, pulled him over the desk, and demanded that he change my grade. A couple of students flew out of the classroom to get the dean of the school.

Dean Wilson rushed into the classroom and said, "Mabel, turn him loose!"

I said, "He's going to change my grade."

Dean Wilson, with authority in his voice, said, "Allow me to handle it!"

I turned the teacher loose, and the dean saw to it that my grade was changed. I never had any issues after that incident.

My mother was fearful that I would get expelled since I "carried my feelings on my sleeve." The school assured her that I would not. The school not only appreciated my parents paying the high tuition and various fees, but they had high regards for my parents and let them know that I was a good student.

I never started trouble, but I did not know how to ignore negative comments that were addressed to me. The old saying "Sticks and stones may break my bones, but words will never hurt me" was the biggest lie I'd ever heard. I never agreed with it.

Mom said, "Stop FIGHTING everybody!"

I'm a work in progress—better than I was, but I still have a chip.

May 1953 finally arrived, and I earned my high school diploma, but my mother told me that she would not be able to attend the commencement. She had a revival at the church, so my brother, who'd just started driving, took me to the graduation ceremony. My dad was unable to attend because he worked from 3:00 p.m. to 11:00 p.m. This was another season in my life of feeling the pain of rejection.

Scriptures to Remind Us that God Will Fight Our Battles

The Lord will fight for you, and you have only to be silent.
(Exodus 14:14, English Standard Version)

For the LORD your God is he who goes with you to fight for
you against your enemies, to give you the victory.
(Deuteronomy 20:4)

But they who wait for the LORD shall renew their strength;
they shall mount up with wings like eagles; they shall run
and not be weary; they shall walk and not faint.
(Isaiah 40:31)

The Lord your God who goes before you will himself fight
for you, just as he did for you in Egypt before your eyes.
(Deuteronomy 1:30)

No, in all these things we are more than
conquerors through him who loved us.
(Romans 8:37)

A Psalm of David when he fled from Absalom his son. O
LORD, how many are my foes! Many are rising against me;
many are saying of my soul, there is no salvation for him
in God. Selah But you, O LORD, are a shield about me, my
glory, and the lifter of my head. I cried aloud to the LORD,
and he answered me from his holy hill. Selah, I lay down
and slept; I woke again, for the LORD sustained me.
(Psalm 3:1–8)

Submit yourselves therefore to God. Resist
the devil, and he will flee from you.
(James 4:7)

Save us, we pray, O LORD! O LORD,
we pray, give us success!
(Psalm 118:25)

When the righteous cry for help, the Lord hears
and delivers them out of all their troubles.
(Psalm 34:17)

For you equipped me with strength for the battle;
you made those who rise against me sink under me.
(Psalm 18:39)

Be sober-minded; be watchful. Your adversary the devil
prowls around like a roaring lion, seeking someone to
devour. Resist him, firm in your faith, knowing that the
same kinds of suffering are being experienced by your
brotherhood throughout the world.
(1 Peter 5:8–9)

Contend, O LORD, with those who contend with
me; fight against those who fight against me!
(Psalm 35:1)

Therefore, take up the whole armor of God,
that you may be able to withstand in the evil
day, and having done all, to stand firm.
(Ephesians 6:13)

CHAPTER 3

When Uzziah Died,
I Saw the Lord

After high school, during the summer of 1953, my parents and I buckled down on the farm, growing acres of vegetables that over the years materialized into truck farming, peddling vegetables from the bed of a truck. Truck farming consists of the daily loading and unloading of the wooden-slat till and half-bushel baskets of vegetables from our acres of garden onto the truck to simply sell from the truck off the side of the roads.

From 1945 to 1953, my parents accumulated eighty-two acres of land. My grandparents, maternal and paternal, accumulated over 200 acres of land each. We grew peas, greens, tomatoes, corn, beans…you name it! During those times, the community defined a well-to-do person or family as one who had acquired a large amount of land, such as our eighty-two acres. Also, if you owned a car, you were deemed to be doing quite well.

By August of 1953, all three of my siblings, Robert, Fannie, and Mozell, were married and had migrated to Cleveland, Ohio, for better opportunities of fulfilling their lives' purposes. My dad saw how well my brothers were doing up North as Black men, so he decided to go to Cleveland and work at their place of employment, Republic Steel.

Republic Steel was an American steel manufacturer that was once the United States' third-largest steel producer. The company was founded in Youngstown, Ohio, in 1899 as the Republic Iron and Steel Company. The company expanded to five other cities in Ohio, Cleveland being one of them.

Although Dad wanted to relocate to Cleveland, he knew my mom was not going to leave her family or place of comfort to live up North. My mom's relationship to her siblings was too close for her to make that move. Dad and Mom compromised and decided on a long-distance marriage so that Dad could make good money working in Cleveland.

On September 2, 1953, the telephone party line rang.

Allow me to interject and say that a party line is a telephone line that is shared by multiple people who can simply pick up their phone's receiver and listen to anyone's call. Unlike the telephones of today, the party lines provided no privacy in communication. They were frequently used as a source of entertainment and gossip, as well as a means of quickly alerting entire neighborhoods of emergencies, such as fires. The party-line telephone was a cultural fixture of rural areas for many decades.

Nonetheless, my mom answered the phone, and shortly afterwards she let out a big scream and was wailing. She got off the phone and told me the news that Robert, my young twenty-five-year-old brother, was crushed to death on his job at Republic Steel when a train went in reverse instead of forward. She continued to say that my sister-in-law was having Robert's body shipped back to Mississippi and that her, my dad, and all the family members were going to be headed back home to Mississippi for a wake and funeral for Robert.

A fear came over me that had me believing I would not make it to the age of twenty-five. My brother was so young. How could this be? How could a young man who loved his wife and a father of two young boys, with another one due in a few months, be gone? There were so many questions that my young nineteen-year-old mind couldn't answer or understand to process his sudden death. Robert's death was so challenging for me and my family; our world was turned upside down. Robert's death was another step in my journey of faith.

Mom began to clean the house in preparation for all her children and their families to return to Mississippi and to make it acceptable for visitors who stopped over to give their condolences. My mother composed herself, stopped crying, and displayed a remarkable strength and sweetness while serving others, instead of being served, in the days before Robert's wake and funeral.

A **wake** is a service or social gathering the evening before the actual funeral service, or what Blacks call the Homegoing service. Traditionally, a wake takes place in the house of the deceased, and the body is displayed during the wake. Yes, Robert's body was in my parents' home, which made dealing with his death even more challenging.

I could not understand death or the turmoil and stress it caused in my home. Although there is no pattern or cookie-cutter formula for grieving, my parents' approach did not appear healthy. They both were in pain; their first born was dead.

At one point, the "blame game" entered our home. Mom blamed Dad for encouraging their children to go to Cleveland and thrive; whereas, my mom, seemingly a controller through my lens, wanted her children to stay in Mississippi, near the rest of our remarkably close-knit family. She argued with my dad saying, "If you would not have encouraged them to go North, my son would still be alive."

In response, Dad argued his point. He was allowing his children to thrive and allowing them to make their own choices. He thought my mother's argument was coming from a woman's emotions, not from rational thought.

As the president of Second New Hope District, which was a youth group composed of all the youth of approximately twenty churches in our district, under the umbrella of the National Baptist Convention, I was supposed to have gone to the National Baptist Convention in Florida to represent our group, but I didn't want to go because of all the family stress after my young brother's unexpected death. The trip was to be paid by the Second Hope District, but my sorrow was too heavy to bear at that time. Instead, that same month Robert died, I went to a local college to become a schoolteacher.

There were not too many jobs available for or offered to Blacks in my community for career choices such as school teaching. Of course, at that time, you could only teach people who looked like you. As a "Colored" woman in those days, I would only be allowed to be an educator for the "Coloreds" or Negroes. The tuition was so expensive. My father really could not afford for me to attend. I did not realize until much later that I could have made it easier on my parents by moving into town and working my way through school. I was not looking for an easy ride, but at that time, I simply didn't think there was any other option but to rely on my dad.

Education in my community was rare because the primary focus was families working together as farmers to produce income and downright survive. As an overachiever, I wanted more than the status quo in my community, and my parents supported me because they wanted more for their children, such as excelling in higher education.

Unfortunately, many people in the Deep South where I grew up, the Mount Pleasant area, averaged only a sixth-grade education and did not celebrate our desire to flourish and soar. The limited thinkers could not see beyond their "normal" everyday life. We were constantly bombarded with negative comments, such as "I do not know why anyone would attend high school or college; they are only going to get married and have a bunch of babies."

Regrettably, I attended college for only a semester and had to drop out in December due to the high cost. I decided to go to Cleveland in December 1953. I stayed with Clara, my sister-in-law, to help her with the cooking and cleaning until her son Herman was born. Herman never knew his father, my brother Robert who died. I'm sure the thought of not having her husband around to witness the birth of their third son was challenging for her, but we never talked about Robert back then.

Recently, without provoking any conversation about him, she said, "Mabel, I think about him every day." Those were precious and endearing words for her to say about my brother, sixty-five years later, and I believed her. I knew she loved my brother, and she has always been a beautiful sister to me. After my brother's death, God blessed her; she remarried a wonderful man who loved my three nephews as his own and taught them so much about being a man. Clara and her new husband had nine more adorable children before his death.

I stayed with Clara for a couple of months and went back to Mississippi in January or February of 1954 to get mentally prepared for the upcoming spring planting time in March. Also, I felt obligated to be there for my parents, to help them.

I never felt right leaving them permanently, so over the years, I went to Cleveland for six weeks in the winter months. I'm not sure what I loved about celebrating Christmas in Cleveland, but I would leave after the first of the year, only to return the following year during the winter.

In November 1954, I joined a church in Cleveland called Greater Abyssinia Baptist Church because I was truly considering staying and making Cleveland my home, but again I went back home. It was hard to break loose from the red clay of the South. Its control over me was so strong I felt obligated to stay. I also felt a commitment to be the one to help my parents in working the truck farming.

Over the years, in the winter months, I would reside in Cleveland for six to eight weeks. I was always blessed to find employment. One of the jobs was cleaning new houses. The houses were newly built, so my responsibilities consisted of washing windows, vacuuming carpets, and washing and dusting all necessary areas to make it welcoming for the new homeowner. Once that job faded out, I began doing day work, which entailed cleaning people's homes for eight dollars per day plus carfare.

Brokenness

I went back home to help work the farm. Although we grew vegetables, as mentioned, we wanted to always have plenty of everything, so we purchased neighbors' crops, the ones we lacked, and sold those along with our crops.

During this season of my life, I was looking for love in all the wrong places and got involved with an older man who was smooth and very manipulative; he claimed the relationship that he was currently in was ending so that he could convince me to have an affair with him. There was no love connection; it was just a one-time fling. I slipped out with him, only to slip up and become pregnant! I did not tell my parents of the pregnancy until I was approximately four months along and had started showing. Mom was very prideful of her maiden family's name, the Sharps, so any sins we committed were quickly blamed on my dad's side of the family. She "seemingly" wanted perfection from her children.

As a member of the Southern Baptist Church, I had to go before the congregation to confess my sin. I was ostracized because of the church's strong stance against premarital sex; my pregnant body showed clear evidence that I'd broken that rule. That No Baby Out of Wedlock rule that forced the woman to be excommunicated was legalistic and not to be found in the Scriptures from the Bible. I was challenged by this double standard that caused me trauma and shame as the pregnant single female, but what about the man? Why the double standard?

The father of my baby wanted to protect his image in the church and his marriage, so he offered to pay for me to abort the child. Of course, with my godly values and the chip on my shoulder because of another rejection, I wasn't going to add to the premarital-sex sin by putting my baby or my life in danger, so I refused his requested abortion that would have been done by amateurs possibly using a coat hanger. I never concerned him again about my child. Being the strong, I-do-not-need-a-man's-help, self-sufficient type of woman, I embraced handling the complete responsibility of the baby.

The following spring, my baby boy, Danny, was born. He was such a handsome, chubby little boy with a rich-chocolate complexion and a head full of jet-black, curly hair. He was not a crier, but a happy baby who warmed my heart and the family's.

Once my body was strong, I went back to working the farm with my parents while my cousin Rosa Lee, who lived in my parent's home, would babysit; Rosa Lee was not able to work because of health challenges. A child having a baby out of wedlock bore a stigma, and back then it was felt that the mother and child should be removed from living under the parents' roof. My dad purchased me a house up the road for eleven hundred dollars.

Farming was from sunrise to sunset. Under the sun all day, the heat draining my energy because of dehydration, I welcomed the weekends! One Saturday evening, the church had a special meeting about possibly reinstating my membership in the church.

Remember, I mentioned that if you had a baby out of wedlock, the Baptist Church would put you out, even if a member of the church was the baby's papa. The men were not accountable for their sins, but the women had to go before the church.

The meeting began by letting the congregation know the sin I had committed. They allowed me to speak before the voting took place. I was very boastful and with strong passion said, "I'm here because it is your rule, but everyone who swims don't drown!" Now, where did I get that phrase? What does it have to do with making a baby? Thank you, Lord, for not striking me down in your church! There I go, trying to correct others and their sins, instead of looking at myself.

After that, the members of the church voted with a vocal yay or nay as to my reinstatement. The members had listened to my frustrated emotions; I was allowed restoration. My parents and I returned home that night and never discussed what was said in the meeting.

The following week was business as usual. The days were long from selling vegetables nonstop; we came home only to pick more vegetables, place them in the wooden baskets, and load the truck for the next workday.

One evening, we went to bed early, as usual, because our days started early. I was so exhausted that evening! I hoped the baby would have a quiet night. At approximately 11:00 p.m., Danny started crying. I said to myself, *I am not getting up. I am going to let Mom wake up and change that diaper.* I lay there, and then I heard his cry get hoarse. Immediately, I jumped out of bed and saw his rich, beautiful chocolate complexion leave his face. I lifted him out of his bed and held him close to me. I knew the worst had happened! I knew he had passed.

Calmly, I told my mom that something was wrong with Danny and that we need to go to the hospital immediately. My cousin Dessie, who lived right down the road approximately five hundred feet, drove us to the hospital because that night my dad was working what we called the graveyard shift, 11:00 p.m. to 7:00 a.m. Also, Mom could not drive the truck because it was full of vegetables to peddle the next day. We didn't think it would be wise to have the vegetables bouncing and jarring around while driving to the hospital in the city, so my cousin Dessie was kind enough to take us in her car.

As we drove to the hospital, my mom said, "He is not crying."

I calmly said, "No, he's okay," even though I knew he was gone. I refused to cry as I held him in my arms, close to my chest.

We arrived at the hospital; I said to the nursing staff in a calm voice, "Something is wrong with my baby."

They took my baby to see what was wrong; we anxiously waited for the doctor to come see us in the waiting room. Shortly, the doctor came out, gently grabbed me, and looked at me.

I told him, "Something is wrong with my baby."

He said, "Yes!"

Mom asked, "What? What is going on?"

He said, "The baby did not make it; he had pneumothorax."

I said, "I have never heard of pneumothorax. What is it?"

The doctor said, "Your baby's lungs collapsed."

I did not react! I was stone-faced! We left the hospital, went to my dad's job at Flintco, and told him the news. I am not one to show sadness or heartache overtly, but the pain was as if I were having surgery without anesthesia. I had never experienced a pain that great!!!

Although I stayed with my parents many nights because of the truck farming, that night I needed some alone time to process the loss of my son. After leaving the hospital and my dad's job, I entered my home and cried out to the Lord saying, "JESUS!!!! WHY DID YOU TAKE MY BABY!?" I cited all the sins of others, "Miss So-and-so doing this; Mr. So-and-so doing that. Reverend doing... Some of the deacons..." I'm telling God about people who are appearing to get away with sinning. I did not have respect for those sinners at church. I could not understand why it appeared as if I were the only one suffering from my sinful choices, and other people in the church who were sinning seemingly reaped no consequences or pain for theirs.

After questioning God and acting as His secretary, pointing out to Him the sins of others as if He were not aware, I actually heard the voice of Jesus say to me in my distress, "BUT I DIED FOR YOU!" His voice was so audibly clear as if a person were in the room speaking directly to me.

I said, "Yeah, Lord, from this day forward, I will live for You! I will no longer grade or measure my Christian walk by comparing my life with that of others." I remembered Isaiah 6:1 of the English Standard Version, "In the year that King Uzziah died, I saw the Lord." I would live for Christ and not measure my life by others and their sins, but truly live a godly life.

The day came of my son's funeral. As a prideful single mom, I was proud to be able to afford the thirty-dollar burial fees for my precious little baby. As mentioned, I am not a person who expresses pain openly, but the tears flowed when I saw the tiny casket bearing my baby.

An elder cousin approached me and in an offensive tone said, "You ain't got nothing to cry about; you shouldn't of had the baby!" She was my elder, but how dare she act in an inconsiderate manner at my son's funeral. She needed some training on funeral etiquette when confronting the bereaved.

I did not respond. The pain was too great for me to acknowledge her ignorance. No one approached me with comfort after her loud statement. I went home dejected—trusting God, but brokenhearted.

One night, I heard the Lord speak to me and say, "Go to Cleveland."

I said, "I cannot go to Cleveland!"

The voice returned and said, "Go to Cleveland."

And so I did...but, first, let's reflect on Mississippi.

CHAPTER 4

Through the Helpless Lenses of Blacks

Blacks worked hard, and as a community we honestly believed the Lord would make a way somehow. We could not be concerned about the lions out there; we had to face them. In other words, we faced what appeared intimidating, seemed oppositional, or caused fear. As a Black person, it was much harder to be as equally employed as a White person.

The White employers would say, "Give the White man the job, and let the nigger seek his God!"

We indeed sought after our God and used what God provided for us, which was acres of land to produce crops. We knew nothing, but God got us through living in the South where there was so much hate because of a person's skin. Slaves in the cotton field would sing Negro spirituals that had a strong Christian theme not only to cope with the pain of being slaves, but also as a way to escape bondage and as a code for those seeking freedom using the Underground Railroad. Being treated as second-class citizens in the UNITED States of America, the melting pot, we continued singing songs, which we now call hymns, in the 1940s to our God for strength and guidance. My mom, who was the song leader of our church, sang a hymn called "When I Can Read My Title Clear." The lyrics are as follows:

> When I can read my title clear
> To mansions in the skies,
> I bid farewell to every fear,
> And wipe my weeping eyes.
>
> Should earth against my soul engage,
> And hellish darts be hurled,
> Then I can smile at Satan's rage,
> And face a frowning world.
>
> Let cares like a wild deluge come,
> And storms of sorrow fall;
> May I but safely reach my home,
> My God, my heaven, my all.

It was these types of songs that encouraged the Blacks to keep pushing, no matter the opposition.

During the 1930s, 1940s, and 1950s, I was exposed to so much prejudice in the South! I remember attending a cousin's funeral; he was executed for a murder that he did not commit. My cousin was a dishwasher at an establishment known as a honky-tonk. This business for White customers was a bar and restaurant in which country music was played. My cousin—we will call him Bobby—was only in his twenties at the time. He was forced by a White man and woman to carry a dead body into the woods; the couple was believed to have done the killing. From rumors in the Black community, it was told that the wife was having an affair, and she and her boyfriend killed her husband so they could be together. That's the body Bobby was told to dump in the woods.

Bobby was covered with blood on his clothes and hands as he was walking the dark country roads to go home after he did what he was told. He was stopped and questioned by police. Of course, his words meant nothing, and so he was arrested for the death of a White male. Word traveled all through the Black community subtly that Bobby was being framed for a murder that he did not commit. You could not react with anger for justice like nowadays. The Blacks feared being lynched or suffering other unfair racist recriminations, so many pretended they knew nothing. You put pieces of the story together to try to make sense of the pain, but it was not a discussion at the dinner table or anywhere. Our men would hold the pain within; it was not common to see Black men cry in those days. Men simply did not cry, at least not overtly!

Bobby's friend, who was a White doctor, grew up with Bobby and knew he did not commit such a crime. He openly expressed his views and beliefs, fighting for justice for Bobby. He was such a bold and courageous young man to side with the Black community, but unfortunately his voice was not heard. We feared for his life, but as a doctor with status in the community, no one bothered him.

My cousin was accused, found guilty, and executed for a death he did not commit. Bobby's doctor friend attended the funeral and apologized for the prejudice and ignorance of his people. The family liked the doctor; they knew he was authentic. He and Bobby were genuinely great friends growing up.

You may question, how did a White boy and a Black boy become good friends when racism in the South was so blatant? Well, Bobby was one of the many Blacks who grew up with White people because the Whites had farmhouses where the Blacks who took care of the land would reside. These Blacks were called sharecroppers, the modern word for slavery in those days; they worked the land, but would get crumbs from the crops. The White owners used the unobtainable-carrot approach, suggesting to the workers that they were so close to getting a larger payout, but had not quite yielded enough crops; they were told they simply had to work a little harder. Many times, the Blacks would work harder only to continue to receive crumbs.

As a Black community in the South, we witnessed so much racism that there was a lack of trust for many White people. It was common for us to go down to the spring to get water, but we were told to never go alone. The adults recommended that we go in threes to avoid any abuse from "the White man."

We would see them approaching us, seemingly looking for trouble, and pretend we saw a snake. We would scream to one another saying, "A snake! Get your stick and kill it!" We would beat the ground screaming. Of course, there was no snake, but this would cause the White boys to run in fear of being bitten by a snake.

Another cousin—we will call her Ann—was a young nurse at Mattihurse Hospital, a hospital for the poor Black community.

She was walking home from work. Two White men were driving down the road, approached her, and asked if she could babysit later that evening while they took their wives on a date. In her young innocence, she complied with their request, thinking of it as an opportunity to earn more money.

They picked her up only to assault her, rape her, tie her up, and drag her behind their car over gravel hills. They tossed her body in a ditch near her home and left her for dead. My aunt, Ann's mother, came home from a prayer meeting later that night and heard a moaning sound. She walked over to the ditch and saw her baby severely hurt.

Ann was rushed to the hospital and was admitted for months before being discharged. It was a long recovery, but she got her health back. Again, the Whites turned a blind eye. No criminal actions were taken, so her mother forced a civil suit. After that, my aunt wanted to get out of the "prejudiced state of Mississippi," and all but one daughter, one by one, moved during the Great Migration.

Around that time, many Blacks began what soon was to be called the Great Migration—Blacks fleeing the South and migrating West, Northeast, and Midwest, looking for better job opportunities in the industrial cities and trying to escape racism. Blacks were looking for their Promised Land where they would be treated as first-class citizens and feel equal.

Today, I can honestly say that my own feelings of inferiority, of being less than the Whites, or of hatred toward Whites are gone. Now, I know that I am okay! The Lord said I'm okay because in Psalms 139:14 it says that "I am fearfully and wonderfully made!" I have learned to TRUST GOD COMPLETELY!

KNOW WHO AND WHOSE YOU ARE IN CHRIST!

For you created my inmost being;
you knit me together in my mother's womb.
I praise you because I am fearfully and wonderfully made;
your works are wonderful,
I know that full well.

My frame was not hidden from you
when I was made in the secret place,
when I was woven together in the depths of the earth.
(Psalms 139:13–15, New International Version)

CHAPTER 5

Fred and Mabel

Prior to my making the big move North, my dad wanted to build a new home for my mom. I helped my dad haul the lumber and bricks. My mother's brother, who was a carpenter, helped build the beautiful three-bedroom ranch home.

After the completion of the home, I packed my things and headed North. This was during the era in which millions of African Americans left the Southern states, where farming, sharecropping, and tenant farming were the livelihood in the rural areas, to migrate to the Northern states that offered industrial opportunities. We made the long drive from Meridian, Mississippi, to Cleveland, Ohio.

I stayed with my sister temporarily; she opened her home for many of the family members who migrated from the South until each adjusted to urban life and was established. My sister recommended that I apply for domestic work—cleaning homes, doing laundry, and ironing; this was the same type of work I had been offered back in the South, common jobs that provided steady work for African American women, unlike the laboring jobs for the men. I was hired the very next day after arriving in Cleveland.

As my sister's home was becoming filled with migrators from the South, I decided to move across the street and stay with my brother until I was able to get my own place. The Glenville neighborhood where we resided was a community of common values and respect for hard workers; the people lent a helping hand within reason.

My neighbor became my good friend. Eloise and I would hang out at her home. Her husband, Charles, was good friends with a guy name Fred, whom women appreciated and considered a handsome man. He was six feet tall, had broad shoulders, naturally curly hair, and a caramel complexion; he was ten years my senior. The four of us would gather at Charles and Eloise's home for card nights. I was a country girl who knew nothing about cards. Fred and I were on the same team playing against Charles and Eloise. Fred, who was extremely competitive, would be so frustrated with my throwing out the wrong card, but he would never miss a card night nor ask for a new partner.

After a lot of card-game nights, we eventually started courting, and the relationship became serious. I was not head over heels for Fred. Due to my past experiences and after working in the South for a taxi company where I overheard conversations of men who had little respect for women, I had developed a zero tolerance for men. I simply was too into me, and Fred was too into himself, not in a selfish sense, but we each had put up walls to protect ourselves.

As time passed, I was ready to find my own place, but my income was not sufficient to afford a comfortable home. Due to my low income, I applied for welfare and asked for housing assistance. I was approved for a home voucher! I told Fred; he did not say much, other than he was going to take the lead in finding an apartment for us. I was naïve and believed that Fred was ready for a stronger commitment.

Fred found a place and took me to the home to see if I liked it enough to reside there. I did. The lady who owned the home asked us to sign the lease papers and then requested my welfare voucher. Fred volunteered to provide it as if we were married.

I immediately told the lady, "Oh no, we are not married! If we get a place together, we will not be using a welfare voucher!"

The lady politely dismissed herself and gave Fred and me some time to discuss the housing opportunity.

Fred said with frustration, "Aw, woman, that's the only way you gonna get ahead!"

Looking at him as he spoke, he appeared to have some form of innocence because he saw nothing wrong with us "shacking up," living together without the benefit of marriage. As the zero-tolerance woman, I immediately said, "If welfare is paying my way, then that is who I'm going to screw!"

He was displeased with my unapologetic, uncompromisingly forthright statement. He was so offended with my comment that he left saying, "Oh no, no one is going to talk to me like that!"

He stayed away for two weeks. I did not care because I had certain boundaries and limitations with a man! While Fred was cooling off or pouting, I went and found me my own home. The place was a two-family house on a street named Ablewhite Avenue in the Glenville neighborhood; I was able to rent the second-floor suite.

Two weeks later, Fred, due to his close relationship with my sister and brother-in-law, found out where I had moved. He came by and asked me to marry him, even though neither one of us was truly ready. At that time, neither of us considered premarital counseling before the "until death do us part" nuptials. Fred believed he was ready to be the provider for us and to build our family.

Fred was the best auto-body repairman in the community; it was a common trade during those days. He took pride in repairing vehicles that had severe damage from automobile accidents or nature's rust. Many people lauded Fred for his quality work removing dents and dings, sanding, smoothing, and providing a beautiful paint job to completely remove all signs of any defects or blemish. Fred worked at various auto-body shops in the community, but never was comfortable enough to consider owning his own.

The Nuptials

One summer day in July, Fred and I exchanged our nuptials in my sister Fannie's living room. The wedding, of course, was small and intimate; the guest list included approximately twenty-five or more family and friends. It was a beautiful sunny day.

I was one to roll up my sleeves and make things happen. No time to be dramatic. As the young people would say, "Just do it!" I was not just the pretty bride, but the chef who used my great cooking skills to prepare soul food for the wedding reception. My sister offered the use of her pretty crystal serving pieces for the food; it was a beautiful presentation.

The common beverage in those days was "punch." It was made in a deep crystal bowl and consisted of concentrated punch, water, and ginger ale to add a sparkling taste; sometimes pineapple juice was added for more sweetness. My friend May Ella, who lived across the street from me, was my hairstylist and decorator. She assisted in converting my sister's large living room and parlor into a chapel. She helped make my wedding day a great day!

The guests were seated and listening to my niece's best friend sing a solo as the wedding began. Fred, who loved clothes and looking nice, was wearing a specially made dark-blue suit, and standing at the front of the living room with Pastor Neal, who officiated the wedding.

My brother Mozell was a comedian, like my parents and me. We were on the second floor of my sister's home, waiting for our signal to come down the stairs. My brother grabbed my arm to take my nervousness away and said, "Mabel don't be scared. I'm just gaining a brother!" We laughed as he was preparing to walk me down the steps and down the aisle to give me away.

There I was, in a beautiful light-blue sapphire-satin dress that came to my knees. I wore that dress for the next three years when Fred and I celebrated our wedding anniversary. May Ella, as I mentioned, was my hairstylist; she pressed my hair with a hot comb and curled it so beautifully with stove curling irons. I borrowed my cousin Birdie's white veil, leaving only a few of the pretty curls exposed. I had on two-inch white heels. Instead of a bouquet of flowers, I purchased a standard-sized white Bible, with "Holy Bible" engraved in gold on the cover; the edges of the pages were gold. I held the Bible to my chest, as if it were flowers, with no shame and for all to see. Both of my parents were proud of me and adored Fred.

When giving me lessons in choosing a good man, my dad would tell me, "Mabel, always look at a man's hands. If their hands look better than yours, keep walking."

Fred was a hard worker with rough hands, chipped finger-nails, and one finger partially torn off. Fred loved my parents. Anytime they came to Cleveland, Fred would purchase them a pint of black-walnut ice cream.

I stood in front of witnesses to exchange nuptials with that man, laughing inside and saying to myself, "I think my parents sold me for a pint of ice cream."

Reverend Neal, who was somewhat long-winded, did the ceremony as short as he knew how. He ended by saying, "Fred, you may salute your bride."

Nervously, Fred saluted me as if he were in the military.

I smirked and said, "Kiss me, fool!"

He leaned toward me and gave me a brief kiss on my lips. No sparks were flying. It was simply two adults committing to one another because they had no interest in dating others. We were both tired of looking for love in all the wrong places. We both brought so much baggage to our union.

Fred was a good provider with a good heart, and I had a vision of being the perfect wife, but our past challenges weren't addressed. We just swept them under the rug, but they would eventually be exposed during the journey of marriage.

Pretty Yellow Flowers

As the days turned into weeks, and the weeks turned into months, and the months turned to years, God blessed us with a total of four girls and two boys. After each of the last three deliveries, Fred would dress in his finest and bring me a beautiful bouquet of yellow flowers. I appreciated those flowers and so did the nurses; they adored Fred as well. They looked at me as if I were the luckiest woman in the world, having that handsome man by my side.

Fred was a great family man. He enjoyed travelling short distances to see his extended family in Mount Union and Philadelphia, Pennsylvania, parts of Virginia, and Detroit, Michigan. I was the total opposite when it came to traveling. I did not mind slowing down or resting from the wifely and motherly duties of a large family. Needless to say, however, Mr. Spontaneous would plan a random getaway and give me less than twenty-four-hours' notice. I would have to pull out a chicken from the freezer, prep it, then fry it, and purchase chips and other snacks for the impetuous road trips. If it wasn't a road trip, he would say at the last minute, "Let's take the family down to the lake for a family picnic."

Yes, cooking was required for these unplanned out-of-town or local trips. Stopping at restaurants multiple times to eat was not in the budget for a family of our size and Fred's income.

And, yes, cooking was also an everyday necessity, but there were some Sundays when Fred knew that I needed a break; he would treat the family to McDonald's, giving each child two dollars to spend. The children would stand in line, feeling independent, and order their own meal with their money; they would take their time deciding what to choose and would use wisdom in their purchasing. No one ever spent more than what was allotted. Most of the time, they would order a Big Mac or Quarter Pounder, small order of French fries, medium soda pop, and a pie. Sometimes, it was a shake instead of the soda pop and pie. Yes, back in those days a complete meal at McDonald's was under two dollars.

Another family outing was a restaurant downtown that was called the Forum; it was cafeteria style. We would dine there on some Sundays as well.

Although I hugely appreciated the breaks from cooking, my love and passion was being a great domestic housewife! I was determined to please my husband by completing my wifely duties before he got home from work.

Back then, clothes were washed with a wringer washer. In case that was before your time, let me describe this device. A wringer washer consisted of a washing basin with either manual or electrical agitation and a roller press mounted above the basin. The tub was filled with soapy water, dirty clothes were thrown in the soapy water, and then the basin was agitated. After the washing was completed, the wet clothes were taken out of the washing basin and fed through the roller press, or the wringer, hence the name of the machine. Then, the clothes were placed in some sort of sink or tub containing clear water for rinsing. After swishing the clothes around manually to remove all the soap, the wet clothes were once more fed through the wringer in order to remove any excess water, leaving them damp, but not dripping wet. The damp clothes were then usually hung outside on a clothesline to dry.

Other tasks that domestic housewives accomplished with pride were mopping and waxing the hardwood floors with Murphy Oil Soap or Pine-Sol; we did this on our hands and knees. These chores to keep the house clean, orderly, and functioning were labeled as the woman's responsibility. Many Black women of my era have had knee surgery due to their domestic duties that, for some, even included going to people's home in the suburbs via public transportation and walking in the cold, wintry elements.

At home, I would prepare with love a hearty breakfast that included two meats, home fries, eggs, and homemade biscuits with coffee for Fred before he went to work on weekdays.

In the evening, I was determined to provide my family with full-course dinners that included a meat, a starch, a vegetable, dinner rolls or cornbread, iced tea or Kool-Aid, and a dessert. Every evening for dinner in our traditional dining room, the children would lay a fresh tablecloth on the rich-wood table, adding ceramic plates—the blue-and-white print that was popular in those days—a stainless-steel fork on the left of each plate and a knife and spoon on the right side, with a glass at the top right of each plate.

I rarely served out of pots and pans, except for the macaroni and cheese or peach cobbler. Everything else had to be placed in some type of glass or china serving dish. Of course, the children would fuss because, as they became of age, they were the dishwashers. Presentation and taking pride in the food for family dinner was important to me.

Fred's routine, when coming home after a long, hard day of work, would be to go up the narrow back steps to bathe and get cleaned up for dinner. Once he came out of the bathroom, he would yell down the steps, "I'm out the tub!" This was my signal to put the bread in the oven. Once he came down the front stairs, smelling and looking fresh, we would all gather at the table to say grace—blessing God and thanking him for the food—and eat as a family. At the end of every meal, Fred would always stand and say, "Honey, dinner was delicious!"

During dinner or any meal, nothing—no television, cells phones or anything—was allowed to distract us or disturb our family's quality time.

Fred purchased for us the big, beautiful home I just described. It was on Pasadena Avenue in the Glenville community. It had beautiful rich wood throughout the entire home, three floors, spacious rooms, and an unfinished basement. In all, we had five bedrooms, and each of the three floors had a living room area, two of which had fireplaces.

Yes, we were the Black *Waltons*, if you remember that television show. I guess the Southern girl in me, who had been surrounded by lots of family while growing up, the Virginia mountain boy in Fred, and the challenges of Fred's childhood, having lost his parents at a young age, all combined to make us both determined to build a strong family. Although we were poor, there was so much love in the Harrison household.

Growing as a Union

Although Fred was Catholic, he started attending my extended family's church called Charity Baptist Church. There was so much love and unity at Charity. As an extended family, we not only worshipped on Sundays, but would sometimes come together to dine, making it a "bring your covered dish" Sunday. Fred enjoyed the family gatherings that were filled with laughter and would always brag about my cooking skills, especially my fried chicken.

I knew the family love and fellowship were the reasons he kept attending Charity Baptist Church. I could tell, however, that he was not spiritually satisfied there.

One day, Fred approached me and said, "I am ready to leave your family's church. They are great people, but I am searching for more, not just for me, but I want more for my children. I want them to utterly understand the Word of God."

I said, "Praise God!" God had already prepared my heart to be ready for changing churches, so it was indeed a confirmation.

Fred said, "I do not know where to go."

I said, "You know that preacher, Reverend Parker, who they call the love preacher because he always preaches 1 Corinthians 13 when he visits our church? Well, he has been trying to recruit people to attend his Bible school. The next time he comes to visit, let's talk to him."

Shortly after Fred expressed his desire to search for more, Reverend Parker visited and invited Fred and me to attend his Bible school.

We decided to take him up on his offer. We were excited to grow and learn the Word of God together as a married couple. We did not know any of the teachers, so we selected the class based on subject matter, not teacher.

Our first teacher had a very monotone delivery. He cited Hebrews 1:1–4 of the King James Version of the Bible:

> *God, Who at sundry times and in diverse manners spake in time past unto the fathers by the prophets, hath in these last days spoken unto us by his Son, whom he hath appointed heir of all things, by whom also he made the worlds; who being the brightness of his glory, and the express image of his person, and upholding all things by the word of his power, when he had by himself purged our sins, sat down on the right hand of the Majesty on high; Being made so much better than the angels, as he hath by inheritance obtained a more excellent name than they.*

I would say to myself, "Will this man please hurry up and quote the verse!" It was torture!

Fred and I were struggling in that two-hour class that had no question-and-answer segment. Here we are, sitting in this monologue classroom setting, and in the room next to us, we hear this loud man teaching and elaborating on the Word of

God with power and enthusiasm. His teaching was coming through the wall. A classmate of ours, Pastor Shell, would press his ear against the wall to listen to this enthused teacher's entire lecture.

We later found out that the energized speaker was none other than Pastor Hawkins, the senior pastor of Good Shepherd Baptist Church. Fred said, "We will have to visit that man's church!"

Although we were attending the Bible study, we still went to our family church. One Sunday, Pastor Neal approached Fred and said, "When I get to preaching good, you walk out."

With love, Fred told Pastor Neal that he enjoyed his teaching, but when he would start whooping, uttering short phrases with a rhythmic quality that bordered on being a musical sort of repetitive chant, Fred didn't understand the need for it. Fred described it as the gravy portion being served after the solid meat had already been eaten. Fred continued and told Pastor Neal that he was feeling led to move his family to a different-style church that was Baptist, but more Fundamentalist Baptist versus Southern Baptist in flavor. Pastor Neal gave us his blessings!

Later, we visited Good Shepherd Baptist Church and immediately felt at home; we appreciated Pastor Hawkins's style of teaching; even our children could understand and enjoy it. During this period, we were focusing on spiritual growth, stepping outside our comfort zone with the family, and creating new relationships with strangers who shared a common denominator—loving Jesus Christ my Lord.

CHAPTER 6

The Village

Community Neighborhood

An intact nuclear family was the norm in our community. The majority of households included the husband who was the primary provider. The wife, in many cases, was a stay-at-home mom who attended to their dependent children and did some domestic part-time work for suburban families.

"It takes a village to raise a child" is an ancient African proverb that means the responsibility of raising a child does not lie with the parents alone, but also with the extended family, and in some cases the whole community—school, church, neighbors, and community centers.

Let us talk about this village by starting with the street where Fred purchased the big home for our family. Pasadena Avenue was a beautiful street of huge homes filled with married couples who had many children. Fred and I had four girls and two boys, and our oldest daughter's children were living with us at one time. Our neighbor the Griffins had five children, and all but one of the other neighbors also had multiple children; one neighbor only had a daughter. Our street was a part of the village for my children. All the neighbors got along and looked out for one another's youngsters.

The street was long and had two parts. The top part of the street was connected to Parkwood Drive, and the lower part to East 105th Street. We lived in the middle, near the dividing street, East 108th, which we called an alley. Being a social butterfly, I connected with so many people on the street. Everyone knew one another on a more familiar level than neighbors today. During those times, I did not mind borrowing a cup of sugar, an egg, or anything from my neighbors, and vice versa. Also, there were no issues or concerns with sending my children into another person's home to obtain these necessary products when attempting to prepare dinner before my husband came home from work.

Pasadena Avenue was family oriented. We would have bimonthly street-club meetings. The street club was what today would be referred to as a homeowners' association (HOA) for all the people who lived on a particular street. The meetings were in different volunteers' homes. The purpose of having a street club on your street was to provide a comfortable approach for creating a friendly community, enhancing a sense of security through knowing that we were looking out for one another, and simply having fun and encouraging one another in different approaches to taking pride in our community, our street, such as keeping our lawns manicured, planting beautiful flowers in our front yards, planting small gardens in our backyards, keeping the paint on our homes looking as fresh as possible, and cleaning up the litter thrown from cars driving down the street. Pasadena Avenue was beautiful and a far cry from looking like a stereotypical inner-city street. We truly took pride in our homes, and people kept their property immaculate.

The City of Cleveland encouraged its residents to take pride in their neighborhoods by sponsoring various competitions, such as Best Yard, Best Garden, and Best Christmas Lights. A dear friend, Lula Dee Wade, had an immaculate yard and would win, or come awfully close, because of her beautiful display of Christmas lights. From the peak to the foundation of her home was arrayed with lights. I never won, but anyone who entered the contest was provided two tickets to attend the city's elegant, formal awards dinner to discover the outcome and view pictures of how the city looked overall, to see the winners and finalists from the various neighborhoods of Cleveland, and to gain knowledge and ideas to make improvements for the following year's competition.

Family Activities

Fred and I were strong on family unity. Fred was raised by his stepgrandmother and other family members during challenging times. He was determined to be the best father he knew how to be since he wasn't raised by either of his parents. His mother, Eliza, died during childbirth in 1926; the baby also died. Fred's father, Raymond, had a lifestyle that didn't meet the approval of Fred's maternal side of the family, so the story has it that they took the children—Fred, his two brothers, and a sister—away from Raymond and called the police so that he would never return. Fred and his siblings were very young and were moved from home to home without the love of parents. They felt tolerated instead of loved.

Fred and I did everything with our children to show love, family values, and unity. Togetherness, family time, was a core value in our home. We did various family activities, such as chores that included, but weren't limited to, laundry, landscaping, painting, and kitchen duties.

Every weekday morning, we awakened the children early in the morning and gathered in the living room for devotions. We studied James and Proverbs. We considered those two books in the Bible as key to setting our children on the right path so, when they got older, they wouldn't stray from our Christian beliefs. We gave our children a firm foundation of our Christian values. Fred had an earlier life of knowing the streets; he didn't want his children to be tainted by worldly values. He didn't allow secular music in the home, card playing unless it was Uno or children's cards that included Matching or Go Fish. Alcohol was a definite no, with both of us in agreement.

Many Saturday evenings after Saturday chores were completed, we would jump in the station wagon and ride to Severance Center in Cleveland Heights to enjoy billiards and bowling. Fred loved billiards, and I loved bowling. As a family, we would bowl a minimum of two games. The atmosphere was so joyous, and there was much laughter watching the younger ones take the heavy balls, roll them down the lane, and only get gutters. Sometimes the ball would roll down the lane, headed to the gutter, but it was as if an angel would reach down and curve the ball for the child to get a strike. Fred and I would laugh as the other children said, "That's just luck." The child bowler would jump up and down in amazement, feeling as proud as a professional bowler. All of them experienced an "angel bowling moment."

Fred would get so tickled to see the joy and love in our family gatherings. Although Fred and I didn't express love with many hugs and kisses, we tried expressing love with quality time.

When Fred and I needed some downtime and the children complained of boredom, he would drop them off at our friends the Wiggins's neighborhood skating rink. The children enjoyed meeting up with their cousins and roller-skating until ten or eleven at night.

Playing family board games was another favorite in our home. Fred loved checkers, I loved Pop-O-Matic Trouble, and the children loved Monopoly and Life. We would rotate to ensure everyone was able to play.

Television was another opportunity for family time. Our living room was so huge that there was enough space to hold our entire family and another family our size. We would gather in the living room to watch family shows, such as *The Waltons, Little House on the Prairie, Hee Haw, The Jeffersons,* and *All in the Family.* Years prior, Fred stopped allowing the children to watch *The Flip Wilson Show* because of our strong Christian beliefs; he didn't want to confuse the minds of his boys and condone a man dressing as a woman. Currently, I thoroughly enjoy Tyler Perry as Madea—he brings so much laughter to the community—but I wonder what Fred would say of the many things on television today.

Also, we attended church as a family. If you lived in our home, you went to church. It wasn't an option. You will read more of this throughout the pages of the book.

Community Schools

The schools my children attended were part of the village as well. I was a highly involved, active parent at the school to show my children that I took an interest in their education.

I immediately became a PTA, Parent-Teacher Association, member. The PTA is a school association run by some of the parents and teachers; its purpose is to discuss matters that affect the children and to organize events to raise money for the various needs of the students.

During the time in which one of my children was attending Iowa Maple Elementary School, Ms. Rhine, who was the principal and a Jew, challenged the parents by saying, "Stop allowing your children to play with clothespins, and give them a typewriter. Teach your children typing! You will need the skills of a typewriter!" She was so right! Today, we use computers, laptops, phones, and notepads that have the same keyboard layout as the typewriter.

The PTA parents were the dress-for-success type. These parents and housewives, who were looked upon as prim, precise, and formal, did not wear casual clothes; instead, they were always dressed professionally and carried themselves with sophistication. They spoke eloquently and never broke the rules of etiquette.

This young lady from the red clay of Mississippi had no desire to be of that type, but my outgoing, friendly personality allowed me to be accepted in such an elite group. Another lady was loud and truly down-to-earth. She and I reached out to the individuals who possibly thought they didn't belong to such a high-society group—the quiet introverts and the extremely outgoing, wild parents—to encourage them to be a part of this association for the betterment of their children and all of the students. Later, because of my outgoing personality, I was voted the PTA Vice President at Iowa Maple. Then, I was able to connect with all the parents, no matter their status.

When you have a genuine love for people and you are comfortable in your own skin, the social status of others is irrelevant. You keep your focus on the main goal—the betterment of the students. We were an awesome group of parents who had dinners at the school as an approach to keeping the parents and teachers connected and working together as a village.

Stephen E. Howe Elementary School on Lakeview Avenue in the Glenville community had a beautiful principal, Mrs. Spencer, an African American who was my friend and mentor. She had a love and passion for the students and expressed it by not only leading a staff who taught with excellence, but going above and beyond by purchasing clothes for the inner-city students and combing and styling their hair so they would feel good about themselves, focus on learning, and avoid the bullies.

Mrs. Spencer had faith in me and gave me responsibilities that I thought required those who had college degrees. She saw in me what I did not see in myself. I became PTA President and was able to develop a bridge for the parents and teachers to work together as a team, creating a strong village to support the teachers for improvement of the children's learning. This was during the time both prayer and corporal punishment were allowed in the schools and parents and teachers communicated respectfully with one another, focusing on the students' best interest and not adult egos. We were successful in achieving a happy medium.

Community Children's Bible Club
—The Big Bible-Club Sign

Jean Wilson, a White, American, thin woman with blonde hair, had a passion to teach in the inner city. She enjoyed reaching out to children, telling them of the love of Christ. Her sweet, quiet spirit had a way of wooing her audience of first- through sixth-grade, inner-city children to listen eagerly to her lesson. If the children became restless, Jean would politely raise a picture of a lady with her index finger over her mouth. Without a word, the boys and girls would become silent for her to continue her lesson.

Jean trained many inner-city parents, such as Marilyn R., Marilyn H., Joceline, Lily, and me, on how to facilitate the five-day summer Bible clubs and the Saturday Bible clubs. Jean was introduced to us at my church, Good Shepherd, where she facilitated our church's weekly clubs. She believed in audience participation to keep the children involved and awake. The children would sing songs, like "Countdown to Blastoff," that provided a Bible verse at the end. The song would get the children emotionally charged to sing loud and with enthusiasm for Jesus. They would stand and start counting down, "Ten…nine…eight…seven…six…five…four… three… two…one…BLAST OFF!"

Immediately, the children would go into singing the full song. Then the children would read the large printed verse at the end of the big songbook that Jean held high in front of the class:

> And if I go to prepare a place for you, I will come again, and receive you unto myself; that where I am, there you may be also (John 14:3).

This was an approach for the children to hide God's Word in their hearts.

Jean also created a fun way for the children to memorize the Pledge of Allegiance to the Flag, the Pledge of Allegiance to the Christian Flag, and the Pledge of Allegiance to the Bible. She would have all three flags in her hand, and each week she selected three students to come in front of the class and hold one flag each. The students would look at their peers at the front of the class and snigger. But with boldness, pride, and voices loud enough for people on the street to hear, the children holding the flags would stand tall and say in unison all three pledges.

Pledge Allegiance to the Flag:

I pledge allegiance to the flag of the United States of America and to the republic for which it stands, one nation under God, indivisible, with liberty and justice for all.

Pledge to the Christian Flag:

I pledge Allegiance to the Christian flag and to the Savior for whose kingdom it stands, one brotherhood uniting all mankind in service and love.

Pledge to the Bible:

I pledge to the Bible, God's Holy Word, and will take it as a lamp unto my feet, a light unto my path, and hide its words in my heart that I may not sin against God.

After songs, pledges, and prayer, Jean would go into her children's Bible story, using a huge flannel board with up to four felt overlays that changed the background on the board. For example, one overlay would be the Red Sea looking normal; the next overlay would be the Red Sea parted down the middle with people walking between the two halves of the sea. Jean would tell the children the story of the Crossing of the Red Sea, while adding to the board stick-on felt figures of men, women, children, livestock, and all their possessions. This style of teaching held the attention of even our hyperactive children.

After the lesson, Jean asked questions about the Bible lesson she'd presented. If a student answered correctly, the prize was a piece of Atomic Fireball candy that cost a penny each in those days. The children would stand, moving restlessly with their hands raised, wanting Jean to pick them.

Jean smiled but kindly said, "You must stay seated and raise your hand without screaming, 'Pick me,' if you want a chance to answer the question."

Although Jean repeated the rules, there were still children who had minds of their own and yelled the answer out or got up and moved side to side with their hands waving in the air.

After her lesson, Jean gave a sixty-second talk using her wordless book; its cover was green. She opened to the first page and held the book up; the pages on both sides were black. She told the boys and girls that we all have sinned, and then she read a Scripture, such as Romans 3:23. She explained the definition of sin and provided examples. She turned to the next page of her book, held it back up, and both pages were red. She explained that the red represented the blood of Jesus Christ who died to cover our sins, quoting 1 John 1:7. Turning again and showing white pages, she explained that if we confess our sins, Jesus will make us pure like white snow, citing Psalms 51:7. She continued, saying if we believed in Jesus and accepted him in our hearts, we could be saved and go to a place called heaven when we die. Heaven has streets made of gold, Jean said while showing the students the yellow pages in her book and quoting John 14:2. Then, she turned to the back cover, which was of course the same color as the front cover, green, and challenged the boys and girls to grow in the grace of God by reading His Word and attending church and Bible clubs. She finished with 2 Peter 3:18. Jean laid the book down on her organized tray of materials and asked all the children to bow their little heads and close their eyes for prayer.

Jean asked anyone who wanted to accept Jesus as their Savior to please raise their hand. The little children squinted their eyes, peeking to look around to see if anyone raised their hands. Jean politely said in a whisper, "Everyone, keep your eyes closed; no one should be looking around." The children immediately squeezed their eyes real tight to reassure Jean that they were not peeking.

After class, we provided the children with two little cookies and a small half-full Dixie cup of red punch.

After weeks of shadowing Jean Wilson and attending training classes, I began facilitating the clubs in my home. The children came in such large numbers that after a while, my pastor allowed us to host the children at the family church next door to my old home on Parkwood Drive. Joceline, Lily, and I rotated classes. We had in attendance as many as sixty-plus students excited to hear of God's love.

To stay current in teaching to elementary students, we became involved with child evangelism training. There was a White couple residing in the Cleveland Heights community who held training classes in their beautiful basement that included a bookstore with all the necessary tools to teach the children. At that time, this was a predominantly White community, but shortly thereafter many Blacks started moving into it, causing another "White flight," Whites moving out due to fear of the Black population growth. The couple closed their home, stopped their classes, no longer to serve and train, and moved out of the community without any explanation. Some of us speculated child evangelism was becoming larger, and someone else would take over their ministry; others assumed they were fearful of Blacks moving in, and still others speculated health issues. We never knew the real reason for their departure.

Nevertheless, we were appreciative to them for their season of faithfulness. Due to them and Ms. Jean, we were able to purchase and learn how to tell a story using the flannel boards, to buy different song books with large print so when we held them up, the students could sing along, and to acquire all the necessary items to make the one-hour children's Bible club presentations of excellence.

Other training workshops and places to purchase Bible-club material were Akron BTU, or Baptist Training Union, which hosted annual three-day training courses, and the Christian Bookstores that were so popular before computers and cellular smartphones provided access to children's story apps and Internet stores.

The 5-Day Clubs used eight-and-a-half-by-fourteen-inch books containing five Bible lessons with five memory verses. The pages were filled with pictures that the children looked at as we told the story, such as the Prodigal Son, the Lost Sheep, and the Lost Coin. Those are just a few of the stories in the Bible that speak of salvation and how God values everyone, even the lost souls—those who don't know Jesus as their Lord and Savior. After that, we presented a missionary story, such as that of Hudson Taylor. We stretched the story out over the five days, telling a little of it each day with excitement and with an ending that left the students thirsty to hear more. We closed each day saying, "You have to come back tomorrow to hear what happens."

The children would make various sounds and comments —"Awe," "Nooooo!," or "Please tell us what happen!"—as an indication of wanting to hear more. This approach made it easy for children to be committed to attending the 5-Day Club faithfully and with listening ears.

The Bible clubs continued for years, including at my home on Pasadena. We put this big white sign on a huge wood post in the front yard's flower bed. With red paint, in BIG, BOLD letters, it said, "Bible Club Today." Since the clubs were held at different times throughout the year, we wrote the next club's day and time on construction paper and taped it at the bottom of the large sign. Anyone walking or driving by could see it.

My children were so embarrassed. They didn't want to be identified as the "Jesus saints" or "Jesus fanatics," but as time passed, some got over it. Others, with no choice, accepted that our house was a house built on "the Rock," Jesus Christ! We were not going to be ashamed of the gospel of Christ!

The Bible Club was a ministry dear to my heart. It was my passion to serve and reach the little ones in the neighborhood. I knew God's Word was reaching out to the community and changing lives in the village; that impacted parents too. God was even using people and churches to donate small wooden chairs for children so that we could accommodate, and have a seat for, every child. Although, we had a long wooden bench on the back row for the older and taller children, the smaller children appreciated having their own individual little chair.

God used my gift as a teacher at a Christian camp in Rock Creek, Ohio, for a week. Sis Norma Hawkins, the wife of Good

Shepherd Baptist Church's pastor, asked if I would volunteer as a teacher. Though it was in the woods, and I would be sleeping in a wooden cabin that only had two bedrooms, each with a private entrance, and a shared full bathroom in the center, I was excited to get away for part of the week. Even though I was raised in the country, I've always had a fear of snakes; still today, I cringe and turn my head if I see one on television. Nevertheless, I took advantage of this offer to do what I love, and the bonus was I didn't have to cook for five days. That was like an all-inclusive paid vacation for me.

My children were there, but they were campers who were supervised by a camp counselor and an assistant. They slept in a large cabin that accommodated ten students of their age or grade level and their camp leaders. They were captivated by days full of activities, such as swimming, arts and crafts, archery, boating, cabin cleanup, and Bible stories, just to name a few of the things on the daily mandatory agenda.

I enjoyed the freedom to sleep, read, and relax without interruptions from my children, grandchildren, and husband. I enjoyed not being in the kitchen to cook three square meals each day and not having to wash or clean up behind little people. This was an opportunity for me to refuel and enjoy myself.

Harry Banfield and his wife were a true blessing to the inner-city children. This beautiful White couple appeared to have an authentic love and compassion for inner-city youth. Harry was the camp director. He sacrificed his summers to be a hands-on director overseeing camp activities. He always had his bullhorn with him, not abusing the use of it but to simply speak to hundreds of children with so much energy and love. He used the bullhorn to gather the children for evening activities, to explain for all to hear the instructions and details for games, like the relay that all cabins competed in against one another. This average-sized, healthy, fit-looking man who was probably my age had an infectious smile. Everyone loved Harry and his wife. They were down-to-earth, approachable people who appeared to enjoy their passion to serve all people of all colors.

The Gregorys, on the other hand, were judged unfairly. I prejudged them and looked upon them as if they thought they were doing Blacks a favor. From the style of their clothing, they looked rich. They walked with confidence, their noses in the air; that was misinterpreted as arrogance. Although they smiled, their interactions with me and some of the other Blacks were short conversations. Mrs. Gregory was strictly business; she had a firm tone as she spoke with the summer camp's paid employees, mostly teenagers, who cooked, served, washed dishes, cared for the ponies, and acted as lifeguards, to name a few of the staff's duties. Little did I know at the time that the Gregory's passion drove them to leave their comfortable style of living and serve for almost four decades as missionaries; that speaks volumes of a commitment to serve others. Years later, I read the following about them on the City Mission website:

> *Angie and Clif Gregory served from March 1948 through March 1985. Angie served beside her husband Clif— one of the Cleveland City Mission's longest-serving superintendents. In her nearly four decades of service, Angie's biggest contribution was founding the Woman's Auxiliary at the City Mission. This dedicated group of Cleveland women did everything they could to meet the needs of those in crisis. They raised money, prepped and served meals, helped with holiday projects, filled baskets to give to the needy, and donated items such as school buses, vans, refrigerators, freezers, curtains, and more.*

The Bible clubs and summer camps made such an imprint on the children that, forty-plus years later, people still approach me and express how they were blessed by the Bible clubs and Christian camp. Many former students expressed either that as a result they had accepted Jesus as their Savior or that their solid spiritual foundation was a result of learning so much about the Bible at those clubs and camps. Some of the students began seeking more and would ask to go to church with us on Sundays to further grow their walk with the Lord.

God's Good News

For I am not ashamed of the gospel, because it is the power of God that brings salvation to everyone who believes: first to the Jew, then to the Gentile. For in the gospel the righteousness of God is revealed—a righteousness that is by faith from first to last, just as it is written: "The righteous will live by faith" (Romans 1:16–17).

CHAPTER 7

Never Lacked

On Thanksgiving Day of 1973, we moved into our house on Pasadena Avenue as detailed in the previous chapter. The happy moments of being homeowners came with the cyclical financial hard times because, realistically, we were not financially stable enough to be homeowners. We stepped out of our comfort zone and went from paying $90 a month for rent to a mortgage of $195 a month.

Although Fred's passion was being an auto-body painter, he had a low tolerance for employers who, he thought, treated him unfairly or took advantage of the great quality of his work by not paying him a fair wage. Fred was not a "give the boss two-weeks' notice" type of guy; he would simply say, "I quit," and leave a company in a heartbeat. I never knew a day of not having that uneasiness, fearing that Fred would quit his job. We were blessed because he was known for his work in the industry; every time he quit one job, he was immediately hired at another auto body shop, but I was concerned that one day we wouldn't be so fortunate. Yet, God always provided, and our home never went into foreclosure.

Spring of 1974, I had to have major surgery. I was not able to cook or do the wifely or motherly duties for six weeks. My mom, Sadie Young, affectionately called Big Mama, came up from Mississippi to help, but so many people would stop in to see the well-loved Mrs. Sadie Mae that the constant high volume of company prevented her from maintaining the schedule that my husband and children were accustomed to for their meals. My mom gave her best in trying to maintain the house chores, even doing the laundry during my recovery from surgery.

One Saturday, she asked my sister-in-law Ruby to assist her with the laundry. Mom washed everything, including blankets and quilts that had not been used in a long time.

Ruby said, "Big Mama, we are not going to wash these quilts with the wringer on the washer being broke!?"

My mom said, "Oh yeah, baby, we are going to wash ev-er-y-thing!"

Mom and Ruby each held an end of the quilts and blankets and wrung the excess water out by hand. After washing, wringing, rinsing, and wringing again, they hung the clothes on the clothesline in the basement to dry.

Ruby laughed and said, "I never worked so hard a day in my life!"

I appreciated them both! I stayed on the second floor and did not come down the steps to interact with anyone until my six weeks of healing were completed.

Over the years, I suffered through migraines because of stress or fear of not having enough and not knowing if we could pay the bills, but we never lacked food, clothes, or shelter. God provided with various means, such as the financial ability to go to grocery stores to purchase food, churches that donated food to us on occasion, and free-food lines to stand in—for example, the one on West Fourteenth where I got meat and other items.

I would send myself on emotional roller coasters of what-ifs. What if one day we cannot buy food? What if Fred loses his job? What If? What If? What If? I cannot tell you when, but God removed that spirit of fear and migraines. To this day, I still must speak in my spirit: "My God shall supply ALL MY needs according to his riches in glory by Christ Jesus" (Philippians 4:19).

I am eighty-eight years of age, and I serve the God who reminds me that I have NEVER LACKED! As Psalms 34:9–10 says, "Fear the LORD, you his holy people, for those who fear Him lack nothing. The lions may grow weak and hungry, but those who seek the LORD lack no good thing."

In 1975, I was diagnosed with pneumonia and recovered. It recurred, but because of my responsibilities to my family, I didn't want to be readmitted to the hospital, so I pushed through the illness.

Although Fred was an awesome provider, I believed my strength as a wife was in managing the home and making his life easier by keeping bills in a mailbox on the wall in the kitchen for him to gather at the end of the month to budget and pay. Also, I called relatives for minor repairs, such as minor plumbing issues, or companies from the *Yellow Pages*—a thick yellow book, which contained a list of all the local businesses, their phone numbers, and addresses—to get estimates for major house repairs.

One day our furnace went out. Not intentionally, I called the most expensive company in Cleveland. I can't remember the actual name of the company, but it was possibly Burns Company, which was located on Euclid and Superior. This company was a godsend because they came out and inspected the furnace, but directed us to apply for a city grant due to our low income. We received a $12,000 grant that allowed us to cut a tree down in our backyard, put in a new kitchen that included beautiful new wooden cabinets and countertops, buy a new furnace, carpet, and wallpaper to modernize our old home. As long as we stayed in the home for twelve years, we didn't have to pay for any of the home improvements.

God, my provider, reminded me of the Scripture Isaiah 41:10: "So do not fear, for I am with you; do not be dismayed, for I am your God. I will strengthen you and help you; I will uphold you with my righteous right hand." Over the years, God continued to bless us! He continued to meet our financial needs, and we continued to trust Him.

August 1979 was a difficult season because our test of faith came not in financial concerns, but in serious health issues. Fred, my husband, was having some health issues. During the night, Fred snored so deep and then would choke, waking himself up in the middle of the night and coughing up blood. I suggested he see my doctor at Brentwood Hospital on the south side of Cleveland. We went back to sleep. I nervously slept, hoping he would be okay until morning.

We awakened the next morning with God's hand of protection over Fred. He agreed to go to the doctor, only to discover later that he had renal failure. Also, they diagnosed him as having too weak a heart to be on the kidney-transplant list. The doctor advised, as soon as a hospital bed was available, that they admit Fred and run more tests to confirm his prognosis.

Fred was a tough individual who rarely expressed his feelings openly. I wanted to sound spiritual and say that, after the news, we immediately held hands and prayed together for a miracle, but we were not that type of a couple. Though we prayed as a family with the children, such a strong test had us going into our own private prayer closets.

Later that evening, we got a call that our second-oldest daughter, Sadie, was going into labor. She delivered her baby girl, but was life-flighted to Metropolitan Hospital on the west side of town due to complications; her newborn was left at Kaiser Hospital on the east side. My oldest son was living with my sister at the time; I called my sister's landline to tell him about his sister's situation and the need for him to come over and watch the younger three children. He graciously came while Fred and I went to the hospital.

As we walked in the hospital, we were approached by a family member of my son-in-law who had spoken with the doctor. The individual told us that Sadie had spinal meningitis.

Calmly, I asked, "Where is she?"

The individual continued to speak about death, saying, "'They' do not think she's going to make it through the night!"

I firmly said, "Where is she?"

The individual continued repeating the doctor's report.

I looked directly at the individual and said, "The judge of ALL earth will do what's right!"

I stepped farther into the hospital to search for my daughter. I approached my son-in-law, who was quiet and had no words to say as he directed me to her room.

There she was…unconscious.

The nurse came in the room and began to cry, saying, "It's so sad that your daughter will never be able to hold her child."

I stood up, hugged the nurse, and calmly told her that my daughter would be fine and healthy enough to enjoy her daughter. I never thought of, or looked at, my daughter's situation as the end. The Lord gave me the words to speak to anyone who approached me with concerns that "she would be all right."

I asked one of the family members to take Fred home so he could get some rest after all the mental and emotional stress and physical ailments that he was suffering from, especially after the report earlier that day. Sadie was his princess. She and her dad had a strong bond, so to see her unconscious, I am sure, was challenging for him. Although, again, we were not the type who openly cried or showed emotions.

I sat by her hospital bed and prayed for hours. Later, I called the various church leaders and prayer warriors, asking for prayers. The first call I made, I gave the information of my daughter being unconscious, and the individual sounded bothered by the late-night call. So I moved on to the next call.

The second call was to an individual who was my daughter's favorite Sunday-school teacher. I said, "Reverend Pickett, you got to get up! We got to pray!"

Reverend Pickett smugly said, "You did not ask me to get up this late at night."

I said with a nervous chuckle, "We got to pray!" I told him the condition of my daughter.

He said, "Sis Harrison, Sis Pickett, and I are going to get up and pray now."

I thanked him! I stayed the night at the hospital with my daughter as I rested on the promises of God.

The sun arose, and my daughter awoke from the coma around 7:30 a.m. With her voice clear, she said, "Mommy, that stuff you got on hurts my head."

I said with a laugh in my voice, "PRAISE GOD!" Mind you, this was a perfume or lotion she loved and had purchased for me. Who cares if her sense of smell had changed? I got some alcohol and washed it off immediately. My child was alive and was going to be able to hold her daughter, just as I had nervously believed. I asked her how she was feeling.

She responded, "I am all right."

I was overjoyed to hear her talking! I called everyone and told them the news of answered prayers!

"My baby is out of the coma."

Reverend Pickett said with a chuckle, "I am glad, Sister, because I intend to sleep tonight!"

We laughed between the praise-Gods!

I went home later that day to deliver the Avon that my two youngest daughters had packaged with the customers' invoices stapled to the individual bags. We got in the car and went door-to-door to deliver the Avon orders to all my customers. Yes, I was an Avon representative attempting to sell Avon as extra income for the house. I became one of the top salespersons in my district and was inducted into the President's Club.

Well, we got through the weekend. Monday or Tuesday, the hospital called to tell us a bed was available for Fred to be admitted on the south side at Brentwood Hospital. The staff ran various tests only to confirm the seriousness of his illness. Fred had renal failure! Brentwood hospital did not have the equipment for prepping him for dialysis or machines to provide treatments, so the hospital decided to have him transferred to Mount Sinai Hospital on the east side. Instead of the ambulance transporting Fred to the other hospital, he volunteered me to take him to the hospital because it was on the east side, close to our home.

On the way to Mount Sinai, Fred asked me to stop at his favorite fast-food place for a Whopper. I said, "Fred, with what is going on with your body, you cannot eat such food."

He expressed how he had been craving the burger for the past three days while eating "hospital food" that, from his perspective, had no seasoning. He insisted on satisfying his craving by assuring me that having one would not hurt. So I stopped at Burger King for him to purchase his juicy, big, flame-grilled-beef burger, a Whopper topped with fresh onions, tomatoes, iceberg lettuce, cheese, pickles, and mayonnaise spread on the huge, soft sesame-seed bun.

He ate en route and…oh, what a big mistake! The medicine he was taking and the Whopper did not agree. He was not one to cry, but he was so sick with severe stomach pain that he regurgitated the sandwich. We got him cleaned up, and I got him to Mount Sinai to be admitted.

Mount Sinai did their own examination, only to confirm that Fred did have renal failure. While admitted, he would have a surgical procedure to prep for dialysis. The surgeon inserted a shunt as an access point for the kidney dialysis machine. In most cases, it is done in the arm by connecting an artery and a vein.

The emotional roller coaster began, commuting between three hospitals to check on my husband, daughter, and granddaughter, plus managing the home and three teenagers. In between hospitals, I stopped at my fast-food restaurant of choice at the time, Church's. I ordered the five-piece dark-meat special for approximately $1.59 and a box of fried okra.

Then, I went to various bakeries to purchase cheap bread and pastries.

I ate half of the chicken and okra between the first two hospitals and the other half between the second and third hospitals. I trusted God but indulged in my drug of choice, which was food. I read my Bible daily, but loved my chicken and bread, whether cinnamon roll or plain white. I hit my highest weight of 321 pounds of emotional eating during this season of running from hospital to hospital.

God was in the blessing business, despite my shortcomings. My daughter improved immensely and was transferred to Kaiser to be reunited with her daughter; she was able to hold her for the first time, and eventually both were discharged.

My husband came home, only to start his dialysis treatments soon after. Dialysis basically mechanically performs the function of healthy kidneys; it filters waste and water from the blood, which helps control blood pressure and the balance of important minerals in the body. The patient's blood is pulled through a filter outside their body, cleaned, and then returned to the body. Fred would go to the hospital for his **dialysis** three times a week for three-hour treatments. Due to Fred's bad heart and complications with his shunt, he was often admitted to the hospital.

Yet, Fred was a tough guy who, I believe, found his sense of purpose through the eyes of his youngest granddaughter at the time. He took so much pride in being a grandfather. From our oldest daughter, we had five older grandchildren whom he loved dearly, but they resided in Detroit and were much older. This new life had come into the world when Fred felt discouraged; he was battling severe health issues, was labeled as disabled, and had to depend on Social Security for income even though he was just in his midfifties. Initially, he was determined to work, but soon realized that the physically and emotionally draining dialysis treatments caused him to be too weak; therefore, he'd been forced to apply for Social Security Disability Income.

My daughter was well and healthy enough to go back to work, so I babysat our new bundle of joy. Although Fred was weak, this little angel was a godsend; she lifted his spirits. She loved her granddaddy, and Granddaddy loved her. On his good days when he felt strong enough, he took her to McDonald's to buy her a treat. They spent so much quality time together, even if it was just watching *The Muppets*. As time moved on, my daughter had another girl, and my oldest son had a daughter. These three little girls gave Fred so much joy and purpose.

One day, I was babysitting all three, and they ran outside to play, only to run back inside to the living room by their granddaddy. The youngest one, Reesie, said, "Kiss the baby," referring to herself.

Fred got so much pleasure from their innocent, unconditional love. He kissed all three, and they asked for more. After a constant back-and-forth, the girls ran back outside.

I was doing paperwork at the dining room. Fred looked at me and said, "Granddaddy tired," and he sneaked upstairs.

The girls came back in the house, stopped, and looked puzzled because Granddaddy was not in his favorite chair. I laughed and told them that Granddaddy went upstairs for a nap. They simply ran back outside and played.

Not only was Fred adjusting to treatments and the side effect of feeling weak, he was also adjusting to his new diet. One day, Fred approached me and said, "Do you want me to live?"

I responded, "Of course!"

In a resigned and weary voice, he said, "Well, whatever you prepare for you and the children, prepare that for me as well. I will eat just a little, but I can't eat the unsalted cheese, unsalted butter, and special foods that you're purchasing at the kosher deli. Please provide me with a little of your regular cooking."

Without challenging his plea, I granted his request. We purchased a blood-pressure kit, and my middle daughter, Freda, and I monitored his blood pressure daily.

Instead of completely resting in God, a light depression and mild fear consumed me at the uncertainty of the "what's next?" God kept bringing us through storms after storms, only for me to fear of the next storm. I refused to allow the depression and fear to cripple or paralyze me to the degree that I could not function. Although I was crumbling inside and eating to ease the pain, I put on my big-girl panties and kept pushing forward to handle business.

We are waiting for Social Security Disability to kick in; therefore, I applied for welfare in the interim so that bills could be paid. The government approved our application and gave us food stamps and a check. I saved as much of the cash as possible, in case of a rainy day, which is what we called a financially challenging day. Also, to keep from losing the house, I went to Consumer Protection; the mortgage was behind, so they advised me to go to Housing and Urban Development (HUD). I went to HUD and applied for a lower monthly mortgage, only to have to wait six months before approval.

Again, God provided financially! He never failed us! The Social Security Disability was granted. Fred was approved for a $357-per month-check. I received approximately $66 per month, and the children, until age eighteen, would receive approximately $59 each per month. That was it, but God used all those checks and multiplied them so that all our needs were met. God blessed and stretched the income by having our HUD application approved for a low mortgage of $50 per month. However, the following year, the mortgage would increase to $75, but that was still $125 less than our original mortgage.

Look at God!!!!!!!!!!!! God has proven to me and my family that He is Jehovah Jireh, the God who provides!

CHAPTER 8

He Is a Walking Time Bomb

Happy holidays!? This is a day to openly express thanksgiving for our many blessings. I wore my smile well and prepared a beautiful meal of plenty for my family. I prepared the traditional Thanksgiving soul-food meal, which included turkey, ham, chitterlings, and all the soul-food trimmings, such as candied yams, homemade, not canned; dressing—no, not stuffing; cranberry sauce, sliced and placed in a beautiful china serving bowl trimmed in silver; greens, collards or mixed; green beans; macaroni and cheese made with the famous government cheese that we called Reagan Cheese in those days because President Reagan distributed it to the poor communities during his administration; potato salad; dinner rolls; peach cobbler; sweet-potato pie; and banana pudding.

Although every day I prepared wholesome, large family meals—which included a meat, starch, vegetable, bread, and dessert, with sweet iced tea prepared with six Lipton tea bags, water, and sugar, or Kool-Aid—and used my Spode blue and white ceramic dinnerware as we all ate in the dining room, Thanksgiving meals were supersized with more food selections and fancier dinnerware.

One thing for sure, as mentioned before, my husband loved and appreciated my cooking. The children, on the other hand, appreciated the huge meal and would go back for seconds, but they were my dishwashers. Instead of allowing the food coma—sleepiness from a heavy meal—to set in, I urged them to clean the dining room table off, wash the dishes, and clean the kitchen. They so dreaded washing all the good silverware, crystal glasses, fine-china plates, saucers, and serving ware used on this special occasion, not to mention scrubbing all the pots and pans. I would hear the children mumbling and complaining as the sound of a metal spatula would strike against the macaroni-and-cheese pan, raking out the stuck particles. I refused to store food in pots and pans in the refrigerator, so all leftovers were placed in Tupperware—the Rubbermaid food-storage containers of those days—and left on the stove in case someone was hungry later. Murmuring and cleaning simultaneously, I invariably heard one of the children say, "Why can't Mom serve all the food out of the pots she used for cooking, instead of transferring it to a special container?"

Sweet-Potato Pie with Some Ham and Chicken

After the children cleaned up, and the kitchen and dining room were spotless, I remember remaining in the dining room, sitting in one of the captain's chairs, from which I could see all the rooms on the first floor. I saw my husband and the children sitting in the living room, laughing and watching television. But here I was, sitting in a huge puddle of invisible tears and having a pity party that no one but me knew about.

The emotional pain of feeling so alone gripped me. How could I feel so alone when my husband and children were within eyesight two rooms away? The pressure of keeping the house afloat consumed me with a wavering faith in God this time.

Our household income had declined drastically because only one child was still under eighteen and receiving Social Security benefits. Also, the babysitting income of my two grandchildren had ceased because they were both of age and going to school full-time. We were on the inversion portion of the financial roller-coaster ride.

I recall staring at the homemade, thin-crust sweet-potato pie I'd baked; it was hardly touched because the family was full from feasting on the other delectable food. In my sorrow, I grabbed a slice of pie and a slice of ham, eating them as I was sulking in my emotional pain. Then I continued to grab slice after slice of pie and meat…until over half of this large pie was gone. I could not just eat one slice of pie; neither could I eat only pie. I had to have ham or chicken with each slice.

I knew then it was time for me to work on me. I had to face not what I was eating, but "what was eating me." I was there full force for my husband, children, grandchildren, and church ministry, but I was neglecting me. I looked strong and happy externally, but I was wasting away internally. At this point, my weight was 315 pounds, and I was developing health issues.

My friend, a neighbor, called me; I shared a glimpse of my current situation of comforting myself by overindulging in food. She recommended that I join a support group called Overeaters Anonymous that she'd recently attended. Overeaters Anonymous is a twelve-step program for people with problems related to food, including, but not limited to, compulsive overeaters. Anyone with a problematic relationship with food was welcomed and provided with a sponsor for accountability. Available for you to call anytime, the sponsor functioned as your accountability partner; you shared your food plan for each day with the sponsor; it had to include three moderate meals with nothing in between.

The following Sunday I joined Overeaters Anonymous and started attending meetings regularly. The group was a blessing for obvious reasons—I eventually lost one hundred pounds by gaining control of my eating—but also because the meetings offered me a moment to exhale and forget about my wife and mom duties. There was a sense of comfort being part of a group made up of people like me. The comfort was not that misery loves company, but it was knowing that there were other emotional eaters out there. Instead of justifying and condoning my overeating, they were a positive support group to help me along this journey of inner healing so that I was strong enough to make better eating choices. That was what I needed during that season of my life.

There again, God supplied, but this time for my emotional well-being! Despite my emotional health, however, the bills continued to pile up. There was simply not enough income coming into our home to make ends meet.

Jehovah Jireh

One early morning, I was in the kitchen, preparing breakfast, and I cried out to the Lord and said, "Lord, you gotta have a way of me going back to work!"

By the time I finished breakfast and served Fred his morning meal, the phone rang. I picked up the phone only to hear Bro Banfield, City Mission Director, on the other end of the phone, greeting me and asking if I would be interested in a position at the Angeline Christian Home, a shelter for battered women. He explained my job duties and hours. He said, "Mae, your hours will be Sunday nights through Thursday nights from 11:00 p.m. until 7:00 a.m. You will enter the new, beautiful, spacious shelter and relieve the second-shift worker, locking all doors, turning on the alarm, only to put on your pajamas and sleep in your private bedroom on the first floor. The ladies with their children will be on the second floor, sleeping or resting because of their curfew. You will not do any intake from policemen on this shift until after ninety days because we want you to feel comfortable in your role. Also, your pay will be $500 every two weeks."

I explained to Bro Banfield our current situation and told him that his phone call was nothing but straight from God. I immediately accepted the position. I smiled at God and shared my testimony to many because, in the midst of my crying out to God, Jesus heard me and provided a job with good pay for not doing anything essentially but sleeping. At my previous job as a lunch aide, I was making $28 per week for two hours of work. To have a job that paid well and offered me the chance to sleep so that I could have the energy to take care of Fred was a blessing from God.

After three months on the job, I would get calls from the various city policemen asking if rooms were available during different times of the night. If so, I would accept the woman and give her the rules of the home; if she needed to talk, I would be that listening ear. I would take her and any children she brought with her to the room where they would reside. The job was that simple. If there was any commotion among the women, I would firmly advise them to get it together to prevent from being removed from the shelter.

God used me to speak to these battered women, to influence their lives by letting them know their worth. God was speaking to me simultaneously, letting me know my worth and how much He valued me and my family. This job took so much stress off me because the needs of the household could once again be met.

God provided! He is my Jehovah-Jireh!

I remember a weekend night when I was happy to be home to enjoy my family, but uncomfortable sleeping in the bed with Fred. Did I become too comfortable sleeping in my bed alone at the shelter? No. This night, Fred and I went to sleep, but in the middle of the night, he sat up with all the covers wrapped around him. I awakened because of the cold draft hitting me; I was freezing.

I did not have to ask what was wrong; the night before dialysis, Fred was always filled with anxiety. Dialysis was so hard on him. This painless procedure took a toll not only because of the psychological battle he fought, seeing his blood leave his body to be purified, but also because of the aftereffects—severe weakness, approximately twenty-six prescription pills per day, and the worries and insecurities about health and mortality that consumed his thoughts well into the nights. He probably kept replaying in his mind the words of his doctor—"Fred is a walking time bomb" due to his bad heart and life expectancy on dialysis—and despairing that he could not be a candidate for a kidney transplant.

After days of awakening to the freezing air, I decided to move into the room next to ours, so that I could get the proper rest to be able to function and see to his needs and those of the entire household. I told him to knock on the wall if he ever needed me. We laughed, and he understood my code language.

As time passed, one night my husband was walking to the bathroom, and I noticed his extreme weight loss and how frail he looked due to the dialysis. He looked so weak, and a voice said, "He will not be here long." I knew it was the voice of God.

Fred was such a private person, even with me. He never talked about anything that he did not have control over, such as death, and I dared not mention death to him. There was only one time that Fred spoke about dying. We were on the porch, and he said, "These children are going to whip you when I'm gone!"

I said, "If they think they are going to whip me, you better take them with you because I will kill them."

His eyes got big as saucers. He asked, "You would not dare think about killing your own children, would you, Mabel?"

I chuckled and said, "Well, you better warn them or take them with you."

That is as close to a conversation about dying that we ever got.

On a warm summer day during the month of June, I was celebrating a major milestone—my fiftieth birthday. Fred took me to Captain Frank, a restaurant downtown on the lake. We had good food and, for me, the greatest conversation that I recall in our marriage. My husband heard me, seemingly for the very first time, as I expressed my hurt, pain, and fears. He apologized for not being a listener in the past. That was my best birthday!

Later that summer in August, months after I saw how frail Fred appeared, he and I were going camping. Oh no, not outdoors, but cabins with beds, running water, bathrooms with showers, and complete kitchens. Although I was raised in the country and worked in the fields, the outdoors does not excite me unless I'm tending to a garden.

Early Monday morning, the day of the camping trip, Fred left to take his dialysis treatment since we were going to be gone for a few days. While he was getting a special four-hour treatment, I had time to prepare and pack our clothing and necessities for the trip. My youngest daughter and I had just finished packing the luggage and cooler in the car; Fred was due home within the next few minutes, and we would be getting on the road for the trip shortly thereafter.

The telephone rang; a nurse nervously told me that Fred was having complications with the dialysis and that I should immediately go to Mount Sinai Hospital. Fred was having his treatment at a dialysis center near University Hospital. I did not understand why he was transported to Mount Sinai Hospital; nonetheless, I did not question their decision.

I then heard a loud voice say, "He's okay; he's with me."

I looked around, thinking my daughter had heard it as well, but it was only for me to hear. Staying calm so no one panicked, I got in the car, and my daughter and I drove to Mount Sinai, only for them to tell me to go to University Hospital (UH). We arrived at UH; the hospital staff put us in a waiting room. I knew then what would come next…

The doctor entered the room and told us that Fred had passed away. I called the rest of the children and told them to meet me at the hospital, where I told them the news and allowed them to view the body. I did not shed a tear! After experiencing the pain of my son's and my dad's deaths, I refused to cry.

I called my pastor and told him and his wife the news. The very next day, they came to assist me with funeral arrangements. We went to the funeral home, and the owner attempted to talk us into purchasing a big funeral by saying it was "what the dead deserved."

I reflected on my dad telling me when he was ill and dying to not allow my mom to spend a lot of money on his funeral. He was a firm believer that money should be spent on those who are alive, not the dead. I was sitting across from this woman, who was the funeral home's owner and director, and planning my husband's Homegoing services, but I was thinking of my mom when she planned my dad's funeral and of my elderly neighbor who had recently asked me to take her to this same funeral home to arrange the burial of her husband. I was familiar with the process, prices, and styles of caskets.

I, a no-nonsense person when it comes to business, told the funeral director what I was willing to spend. She then offered me a cheesy-looking brocade casket for $1,382. Immediately, I stood up and said, "Oh no, we will not put him away like that. We can shop around; he ain't going anywhere!" I started walking toward the door.

My pastor, who looked baffled by my abrupt move to leave, said, "Sis Harrison?"

I said, "It has not been too long ago that a nicer casket was offered to my neighbor for a better price."

The lady, clearly frustrated, said, "Come on back. We can look at something else."

I followed her, and she offered the steel-blue casket that I wanted. She then said, "Well, if you get this one, you will not get an escort."

I firmly said, "You mean to tell me that we will not have an escort from Good Shepherd Baptist Church, off Euclid Avenue near Torbenson Drive, to Riverside Cemetery that is on the west side?"

She replied, "Well, just one!" She went through her itemized list, even tacking on fifty dollars to pay my pastor to eulogize the service.

Immediately, I said, "You can erase that!"

My pastor, with a chuckle, looked at his wife and said, "Sis Harrison does not want them to pay me."

I laughed and reminded him that he'd told Fred and me, if we joined his church and if we were faithful, he would marry us or bury us. I then chuckled again and said, "I am not getting married, so bury Fred."

My sister, who was with me, and the pastor's wife laughed.

In the end, I managed to purchase the complete funeral package for $1,382. That included a family car, escort, casket, and burial. I purchased the casket spray from my friend's daughter who made beautiful flower arrangements. The repast and programs with Fred's picture on the front were provided by the church.

The day of the funeral, the church parking lot was packed with so many cars that even the escort could hardly get in the parking lot. He immediately called for assistance. We were able to have two escorts, with no extra charge.

Overall, the funeral was not hard to sit through because you are in a daze. You see but do not see people. Fred and I were Fundamentalist Baptist, so the style of the service was not too conservative—as a Catholic church setting is—but it was not to the extreme of a high-energy, holy-dancing Pentecostal Church service. Neither did it have the country-church, long-winded preacher flavor. Fred's service was scheduled for no more than two hours, which included thirty minutes for greeting the family. We did the traditional service—the family walking into the church together, following the pastor who quoted Bible verses until we reached the casket at the front of the church.

I stood at the casket and focused on every one of my six children and eight grandchildren as each viewed Fred. I wore the traditional black dress and hat, but no veil. I looked down at my husband's empty shell, knowing he was in heaven. We sat on the front row and were greeted by many people. The line of people seemed endless. The actual service began with prayer, a reading from the Old and New Testaments, and selections from the choir and solos. Let the "show" begin.

As I mentioned, we were Fundamentalist Baptists. Before the funeral, Fred's nephew asked if he could sing at the service. He was from out of town; I granted him his request to sing at his uncle Fred's funeral. He sat down at the piano and began with Sam Cooke's song "A Change Is Gonna Come." We looked at one another with embarrassment. Although we laugh about it now, it was an extremely uncomfortable moment in our church. That song was considered too worldly to be sung in our church during those days.

We got through that, only to have a different reaction to the men's choir; Fred's friend led the songs with so much enthusiasm and energy he went down on one knee as if he were Elvis. I noticed my children's smiles and light giggling; they were being highly entertained. This was a moment to exhale and know they were going to get through the day.

Our pastor did a short twenty- to thirty-minute eulogy, and we were dismissed to the singing of Fred's favorite songs, "Never Alone" and "When We All Get to Heaven!" There were so many cars in line to go to the burial site. We finally got to the cemetery for the quick three-minute conclusion of my husband's service.

The repast was at my home, so I was able to be in comfortable clothing and escape to my bedroom to breathe. I wanted my children to be able to escape as well. Although the line was down the street for people to enter my home and get a plate of food, my focus was on the comfort of my children and me.

Unfortunately, I suppressed the tears only to revert to my old bad habits of overindulging in food. As I masked my pain, thinking I needed to be strong for the children, over a short time I gained back the one hundred pounds I'd lost, plus more. Although all my children were grown, except my youngest daughter who was going into her senior year of high school, I thought I needed to be the rock as they were experiencing the grief of losing a parent.

Spring of the following year arrived; a family friend came to my home and said, "Mabel, you ain't married yet?"

I said, "Child, when I see a man coming from the corner of my street, headed in this direction, I start rubbing with Sloan's Liniment or Ben-Gay." Ben-Gay is an arthritis medication with a strong scent. "I am not looking for anyone, and I don't want anyone looking for me!"

He said, "Mabel, you are still a fool!" We laughed, but I was serious.

I never looked at my situation as a single mom until one day I was walking out of the house, and it came to me—*he is gone*. I asked God to keep me pure. I was so protective of my daughters and had no desire to bring a man around, one who would be goody-goody to me, but pat my girls' butts behind my back. I was not ready to go to prison.

Over thirty-five years, God has kept me. I have no regrets! Some may look at it as if I made the sacrifice to protect my daughters, but it was even bigger than that. It was a sacrifice to live for Christ. I HAVE NO REGRETS!

CHAPTER 9

Teamwork Makes the Dream Work

My oldest son, Ted, thought it would be helpful for him to move back home soon after Fred's funeral. My two sons, Ted and Freddie, and I came to the table to see how and what was needed financially to sustain us and keep the house going after Fred's death. My two daughters and my two sons who resided with me all contributed financially to ensure the mortgage and all house bills were paid. The utilities were never cut off! My children came together, and we worked closely as a team to ensure I'd never lose the home due to foreclosure.

Fred's death drew us so close. Despite the pain of the children being without their father, we were there for one another. My youngest daughter, Lori, was in her senior year of high school. Our house was full of LIFE. My youngest son's friend, Jay from New York, who was attending college here, needed a place to stay. My huge home was big enough to accommodate him. He had his own room and shared the third floor and its full bathroom with my sons. Yes, he contributed to the bills as well. He blended in with the rest of my children.

I continued enforcing the house rules after Fred passed—no alcohol, no drugs, no cohabiting, and no staying out all night if you lived under my roof. All the children, including Jay, respected the rules.

My youngest son, Fred Jr., took after me; he was outgoing and had so many friends who would gather at the house for NFL football parties and boxing matches. This was during the time when Mike Tyson was the Heavyweight Boxing Champion; he would knock a fighter out before the first round of wings or popcorn was consumed. We made jokes anytime there was a Tyson fight, such as, "Do not go to the kitchen to get refreshments or blink, or you will miss the fight." He was known for knocking guys out in the first round.

I would sit in my favorite chair in the dining room and watch my young-adult children and their friends interact. Our home was full of so much positive energy and laughter. Allow me to interject to encourage young parents to enjoy the laughter and noise of your children because it will steadily fade into the distance as each child becomes their own person. As a woman in my eighties, I have become used to being alone, but many days I miss hearing the constant laughter of a house full of folks. The children joking with one another, the competitive spirit during NFL football games when some family members cheered for the Cleveland Browns and others cheered for the opponent, such as the Pittsburgh Steelers, Detroit Lions, or New York Giants, the high fives and celebrating victories of their winning team, and the laughter at simple things—all of that did my heart good. The love was overwhelming and a blessing from God. I appreciated their love and respect for me and each other.

Lori's high school senior year concluded; her final grades were As and Bs. Fred's death did not affect her grades, but right near graduation she was looking for love, seemingly to fill the void left by her father's death. Her high school graduation day arrived; I enlisted a strong support group of family members to attend her graduation. She was the only child who did not have their father present at the commencement.

This was the first time I shed tears after Fred died. I said to myself, *I wish he were here to see his last child graduate from high school*. But as you know by now, no one saw my tears. I put on my big-girl smile and attempted to be strong for Lori and the rest of the family.

Graduation day was great, but I noticed there was a young man who had Lori's heart. Well, this young man, whom Lori started dating that summer before attending Kent State University, was a member of our church, Good Shepherd Baptist Church. Would this be a distraction from her focusing on school and obtaining her degree?

She completed her first semester after struggling in her classes and getting low grades. I asked her about her plans. Without any argument, she went back the next semester, but the same patterns repeated. She came home every weekend, her study habits were not serious, and the bulk of her free time was with this young man. A few weeks before finals, she packed her things at Kent State, dropped out of college, and came home.

One Sunday afternoon, she and her friend wanted to meet with me. We sat at the dining room table, only for her to tell me the dreaded news that she was pregnant. Immediately, defensively and probably out of fear that I would be upset and kick her out of my home, she said, "We're going to do the right thing!"

Calmly but sternly, I said, "What is the right thing?"

She said, "Get married!"

Without hesitation, I said, "You do not get married just because you are pregnant! Marriage is a major adjustment all on its own; adjusting to a newborn at the same time will be quite the test. If you are only getting married because you got pregnant, you need to rethink that major decision."

Over time, after hitting a wall and not being able to convince a teenager who was determined to marry, I let go and prayed much. I was not the type to get upset and throw any of my children's confessed sins in their faces. I knew they were dealing with their own convictions, as I had dealt with my past sins.

Later, the siblings found out the news. Her youngest brother, Freddie, openly opposed the marriage. Lori still could not provide any solid reasons for wanting to get married, other than she was pregnant and "wanted to do the right thing."

Lori and her friend scheduled a marriage date for November 14, 1987. It seemed as if this was the season of my four youngest children taking their relationships with their friends to a new, more deeply committed level.

The wedding bells began to ring, starting with my middle daughter, Freda. I loved her husband. He was like a son and had a great work ethic. He was welcomed into the family with open arms by everyone. They lived with me after their nuptials. They had a small, intimate house wedding, just as I did. Their colors were red and white. Her beautiful white wedding dress was made by my sister-in-law, Pearl, who was an awesome seamstress and could sew and design anything you requested. She did three of my daughters' prom gowns and wedding gowns.

Freddie's wedding followed with a traditional church wedding, colors of gray and pink, and a large wedding party. Ted's was a small, beautiful house wedding with colors of white and peach.

Well, two weeks prior to Lori's wedding, she decided to call it off. Who cared that her beautiful off-white-lace gown paid for by her sister, wedding announcements, and other purchases by family members specifically for the wedding wouldn't be used? I knew she and her friend were not ready for the covenant of marriage, and I was glad that God had opened her eyes.

Well, both of my youngest daughters were pregnant at this time. Besides Fred's death, nothing scared me more. I thought to myself, *What are you going to do now? How are you going to handle this new challenge?* I was terrified because I kept recalling an incident in my past.

A few years before, I heard that my cousin was in Suburban Hospital, fighting cancer and unable to move from her hospital bed. Her daughter was pregnant, and the fetus was full-term; she was across the bridge in Brentwood Hospital. This young lady was told that her baby was dead inside of her. The doctors told her that they would not induce labor;

they wanted her to go into natural labor. My heart was so heavy when I heard the news; I rushed to the hospital to be with the young girl. It was painful to see her separated from her mom, unable to turn to her mother for advice and guidance, yet the only thing keeping them apart was a bridge that connected both hospitals.

I prayed for strength and God's comfort for her. I was there as an older cousin to see this helpless young lady give birth to a deceased baby whom they allowed her to hold on her chest. The image of her holding her deceased baby will be etched in my mind forever.

Now, to see my two youngest daughters pregnant and on bed rest, per doctor's orders, had me so concerned, but I emphasized to the girls the importance in following doctor's instructions. I didn't mind going up and down the steps to provide their meals if that would ensure their babies would be born healthy. This was during Freda's third trimester, but Lori was early on in her pregnancy. After a week or so, Lori refused the care. She is my prideful child who had issues being served meals.

Instead of getting upset, I prayed for both daughters. Praise God, they both had healthy babies, and our family continued to grow with more grandchildren. All my sons and daughters had children, except my youngest son and his bride. Three of my grandchildren lived in my home with their parents, and the others came over quite often.

My home continued to be filled with love and laughter. All my children, except Lori, were now married. I felt close to my sons-in-law, but my daughters-in-law were a bit stand-offish. My sons and I had remarkably close relationships, and they were there for me at a call. Seemingly, my daughters-in-law could not understand the mother-son bond, but as time passed my two daughters-in-law figured me out and loved me unconditionally, and I loved them. We developed a close relationship. I never had any major issues with my in-laws because I tried to be a mother and mother-in-law who did not take sides, but who stayed out of all my children's business.

Did my children and in-laws have flaws? Absolutely! If anyone wanted to talk about their spouse, I was their sounding board, but one who directed them to the Word of God. I tried to take a neutral stance and allow God's Word to speak.

My God-given gift is to love and encourage people. God allowed the pain from various rejections in my life to fuel my journey of loving people unconditionally and ministering to their needs. To this day, I don't think I'm better than others, but I have always been comfortable in my own skin. As a brown-skinned, short, and heavyset woman from the Deep South of Prejudice, Mississippi, I never allowed anyone to make me feel less than they, whether White, rich, college educated, skinny, tall, or whatever difference between us; I never felt inferior.

People gravitate to me because of my smile, which is inviting, but I believe that, once they communicated with me and got to know me, they appreciate how REAL I keep it! The sugar-coating is only transferred by my smile, but the actual words that I speak are directed with truth from God's Word. As the old folks would say, "I tell it like it IS!"

My children's friends would come around knowing that alcohol and drugs were not allowed, but God's "down to Earth" love saturated our home. It wooed people to come over and hang out at my house. The atmosphere was full of so much joy and laughter. Once, someone made a statement about how they were surprised to see a family have so much fun without alcohol. Natural, sober fun!

I genuinely enjoyed all who came over to my home. Even when most of the children were grown, married, and gone, my home was a central location for good, clean fun. God used me as a vessel to speak in the lives of so many young people. They even attended church with me to see and hear about this Jesus who placed a genuine natural smile on my face.

Oh, let me not forget to mention that the fellows—that's what we called my youngest son's friends—enjoyed our special-occasion meals. One fellow liked to open his jacket with a big smile and show me his shining silver spoon, fork, and knife. We all got a kick out of silly Ricky coming through the door saying, "I came prepared!"

Lifted High Off the Ground

A few years passed, and one Friday evening in August 1990, Lori and I were relaxing in the living room when my youngest son, Freddie, stopped over to visit and pick up something I'd borrowed from him.

At the end of his visit, he said, "Mom, do you have the twenty dollars I loaned you?"

I said, "No, but take my card."

He took it hesitatingly and began to walk toward the door, only to turn back around and give me the card back. Gently, he said, "Don't worry about it." He got in his car and drove to his house, which was less than five minutes away.

Across the street from Freddie's home was a playground. He saw his neighborhood friends playing basketball. Freddie was just recovering from food poisoning. He was off work for almost a week, but the doctor gave him the green light to go back to work the upcoming Monday. He decided to join the guys on the court and play a game. They selected their teams, and everyone was talking smack about which player was weak in his game or which team would win. As the game progressed, Freddie had the ball and was dribbling it on the concrete. All of a sudden, he stopped and sat on the pavement, clutching the basketball, and then he lay back on the ground.

His friends said, "Man, stop playing! Get up!"

He would not move!

They realized that something was not right! Cell phones were not common in those days, so one of his friends ran home, which was right next to the playground, and called 911. Then he had his mom call my neighbor, whom she was friends with, and ask the neighbor to call me.

My neighbor Rose called and said, "Mabel, Freddie passed out on the playground."

Lori and I immediately got in the car and rushed over to see my lifeless son on the pavement. The EMT workers were trying to resuscitate him by sending electric *shocks* to the heart muscle as his body was lifted high off the ground, but there was no sign of response. They rushed him to the hospital.

Lori and I got to the hospital, and all the siblings, Freddie's wife, and his best friends, the fellows, trickled into the hospital. The doctor came out to tell us the unsettling news that Freddie had died, but I already knew he'd "checked out" when I saw my baby motionless on the playground. The doctor's confirmation just made it a reality to "encourage myself in the Lord" to go into "strong Mom mode" for my children.

Shortly after Freddie's death, I was not surprised that the phone calls would lessen, the sympathy cards would vanish, and visits from so many friends and family would cease within two weeks. Less traffic from people was common, and my experience with Danny's and Fred's deaths prepared me for the extreme quiet after the burial.

During the quiet moments, I reflected on my Freddie. Allow me to share a brief window of this incredible son whom God entrusted me to instruct, guide, and counsel for twenty-three years as a parent. He was so much like his father in many areas. He had a great work ethic, and although he knew his father's trade, Freddie decided, after attending a junior college in North Dakota on a partial football scholarship, to venture into working at a fiberglass factory. There, he worked long hours to ensure his and his wife's bills were paid.

He was a responsible provider who liked nice things. His home décor had beautiful modern furniture and was always tidy and nice, giving equal credit to his wife who was exceptionally clean and organized. He was the typical young man who loved a nice, shiny toy. He had a beautiful black Cadillac Eldorado that he kept clean, polished, and shiny.

BUT what was most special about Freddie was that he stepped up as the man in the home and showed great leadership skills when my husband died. He had a sincere heart, and he made sure I was all right at all times. We had a special bond. He was such a caring person who was firm with business matters when finance issues or decisions arose that required a male influence. He never disrespected me in any situation, even if we did not agree on an issue.

We laugh to this day about how Freddie was the baby boy, but he spoke to his siblings in an authoritative manner, just as his father would have. Although under their breath they may murmur, "He ain't my daddy," they all had the utmost love and respect for him. He truly was family oriented and simply wanted what was best for the whole family. He had such high regards and a genuine unconditional love for me that when God took this special child, I needed God to give me an "it is well with my soul" peace about my Freddie being gone.

One night, God allowed me to dream a dream that seemed so real. The dream was a gentle tap on my shoulder by Freddie's hand and his deep voice saying, "Mom, don't worry; I'm all right!" God gave me the peace I requested; although Freddie was absent from his body and this Earth, he was indeed present with the Lord! God loaned me Freddie for twenty-three years. I must surrender him back to God.

Once again, outwardly, I felt the need to keep my emotions under control, but I was overindulging in food. I needed psychological help to get me through this pain that I was suppressing with food. The one hundred pounds, which I'd previously lost, gradually returned with an additional six pounds, bringing me to a weight of 321 pounds. I went to my primary doctor, who was a Christian, and asked him to refer me to a therapist.

He said with a big smile, "You do not need a psychologist!"

I told him, "I need something! I need help!" Yes, tough Mabel, who was there for everyone else, was crumbling inside.

I was assigned to Dr. Graham; she was a jewel of a counselor. God used her to get me through the accumulative losses and other difficult seasons in my life.

Scriptures for Comfort if Grieving the Loss of a Loved One

- *For the Lord will not reject forever, for if He causes grief, Then He will have compassion according to His abundant lovingkindness (Lamentations 3:31–32 (New American Standard Version).*

- *The righteous perish, and no one takes it to heart; the devout are taken away, and no one understands that the righteous are taken away to be spared from evil. Those who walk uprightly enter into peace; they find rest as they lie in death (Isaiah 57:1–2).*

- *Fear not, for I am with you; be not dismayed, for I am your God; I will strengthen you, I will help you, I will uphold you with my righteous right hand (Isaiah 41:10).*

- *Peace I leave with you; my peace I give to you. Not as the world gives do I give to you. Let not your hearts be troubled, neither let them be afraid (John 14:27).*

- *He will wipe every tear from their eyes. There will be no more death or mourning or crying or pain, for the old order of things has passed away (Revelation 21:4).*

- *I have no one else like him, who will show genuine concern for your welfare (Philippians 2:20).*

- *For this God is our God for ever and ever; he will be our guide even to the end (Psalm 48:14).*

- *Blessed be the God and Father of our Lord Jesus Christ, the Father of mercies and God of all comfort, who comforts us in all our affliction so that we will be able to comfort those who are in any affliction with the comfort with which we ourselves are comforted by God (2 Corinthians 1:3–4).*

- *Therefore you too have grief now; but I will see you again, and your heart will rejoice, and no one will take your joy away from you (John 16:22).*

- *The LORD also will be a stronghold for the oppressed, A stronghold in times of trouble (Psalm 9:9).*

- *God is our refuge and strength, A very present help in trouble (Psalm 46:1).*

- *O death, where is your victory? O death, where is your sting (1 Corinthians 15:55)?*

Additional Photos

Children's Weddings in order of Nuptials

Sadie and Mickey's Wedding   Gwen and Fredd's Wedding

Freda and Thomas's Wedding   Fred Jr. and Pequita's Wedding

Ted and Terri's Wedding

Lori and Nevin's Wedding

Families of Fred and Mae's children

Gwen's Clan

Sadie's Clan

Ted's Family

Freda's Clan

Lori's Clan

ME WITH MANY OF MY CHILDREN
and GRANDCHILDREN

CHAPTER 10

It's Bigger than I Am

I stayed engaged in the church. Some people take a sabbatical after losing a loved one, but I'm an extrovert, and I needed to be around other people and in an atmosphere of spiritual worship. So I attended my church, Good Shepherd, regularly to stay connected with my friends and, more importantly, to get spiritually fed and have that "blessed assurance" that Jesus had me even in this season.

I continued to serve as a Sunday school teacher for the women. Our classes were full of discussions as we dove deep into the Word of God. My best friend, Maggie, whom I called "my nutty buddy," was my co-teacher. We rotated or sometimes tag-teamed during the class. If she had a strong point during the class, she would interject. We had a smooth flow for keeping the ladies engaged and excited about hearing God's Word.

Maggie was special and a dear friend. We had so much in common. She was country, but from Georgia; I was country. Our husbands were both leaders in the church. We had large families, and our children were close in age.

What made us super close was we both loved Goodwill shopping and yard sales. Yes, secondhand shopping was the highlight of the week. We shopped on Thursdays and sometimes Saturday. We drove out into the suburbs looking for yard-sale signs, only to hit the brakes and make an exciting, godly U-turn. She loved finding designer clothes, and I looked for quality houseware items, such as a good cooking pot or roasting pan, anything to enhance my cooking skills.

When my husband was alive, she knew the name brands, so she would make suggestions on what dress shirts to purchase for him. Fred loved looking good, so Maggie's ability in selecting fashionable clothes for Fred and my strength in cooking and sending her husband my famous sweet-potato pie or candied yams allowed our husbands to appreciate our friendship.

After almost fifty years of friendship, we talked on the phone often. She called, and her first words were usually "Why are you on my mind? Are you okay over there?" Her favorite thing to call someone is fart, and instead of no, she said, "I don't wanna." Our bond was tight! We both buried our husbands, we both buried a child, and we both lived to be over eighty-five. Our common saying is "Getting old, it ain't for the weak."

As mentioned, one of my specialties in baking is a sweet-potato pie. Saturdays, I would bake little sweet-potato tarts, whole pies, and peach cobblers to sell after church on Sundays. I never brought a pie back home. Those pies would sell so fast, and the positive feedback kept me encouraged to be consistent every weekend; it also supplemented my income.

My friend Marsha owned a restaurant; she had her sons purchase the pies, which she resold at her restaurant. She and my daughter Lori recently reminisced about how she would order three or four pies, but by the time the boys made it to the restaurant, a pie was always missing. They would devour it en route. Another friend expressed how her husband loved my pies. She recently commented "oh how" they missed my pies and said that I needed to reopen my kitchen for pie baking.

I guess my love language would be "words of affirmation" because I get so much joy from hearing the funny pie stories and seeing the smiles and excitement of the people who express pure satisfaction when remembering them.

Another ministry that I thoroughly enjoyed was visiting nursing homes and caring for the elderly. It was one of my life-affirming ministries that was a godsend outlet—serving and pouring kindness into people who were lonely, had few visits from family, or were unable to care for themselves. Visiting people at the various nursing facilities gave me a purpose and a sense of worth. They were just simple gestures—bringing candy, sweet-potato tarts, or a small individual loaf of pound cake that my sister-in-law Maggie B. made with all homemade ingredients. Spending quality time with the residents as we exchanged laughter and reminisced about our pasts was appreciated by all of us. The same stories were sometimes repeated; nevertheless, we laughed as if it were the first time being told.

I was in my element in fellowshipping with these special, adorable old acquaintances who just wanted a genuine touch, a friendly smile, and heartfelt love. I received more from them than I gave because the visits allowed me to stay busy and to focus on the needs of other people, rather than dwelling on my own pain by soothing it with food. Life is bigger than I am and bigger than my speed bumps, which come in the form of life's challenges.

If I may, I'd like to reminisce about where my caring for seniors originated. When Fred was alive, we visited my cousin who was very ill back home in Meridian. I remember when we got to the country yard of her home, the odor was so strong. We entered the home to see her lying in her own bodily fluids from the shoulders down.

Fred and I were protective of our elders and wanted to make sure that they were cared for properly and that innocent children were cared for and had quality meals. We went to town and purchased sheets. I bathed my cousin, rubbed Vaseline, white petroleum jelly, on her body to protect her skin, washed down the bed, and made it back up with dry linen. Adult pull-ups were not yet available at that time. The mattress was protected by a plastic shield.

My cousin could not speak due to a form of dementia, but she smiled as a nonverbal gesture to show her appreciation.

When I was a young person, I was the one whom my mom would send to see and care for family members in the nursing home or at their own homes. I would read the Bible to them and care for them however needed. I thoroughly did not mind my mom volunteering me to serve the elders.

Another passion was working as a hospice volunteer. Hospice care is taking care of terminally ill patients; it centers around managing their pain and symptoms, making them comfortable, and attending to their emotional and spiritual needs at the end of life. One day, a member of the Western Reserve Hospice staff called Sis Griffin, the charity organizer at Good Shepherd; Sis Griffin recruited church members as volunteer hospice caregivers. The hospice staff member expressed her desire to have me on board as a volunteer. She indicated my natural God-given gifts—an authentic warm smile that was inviting and a natural caring and comforting spirit. She went on to say I would be a highly desirable addition to her team due to how she had observed the nurses on her staff studying how I was with the patients. Apparently, they'd paid attention to how I interacted with people in the halls of the facility and with my close friend Marilyn who was in the hospice at the end of her life. She had four sons who never wanted her to be alone, so they asked me to sit with her when their schedules didn't allow them to be there.

Unfortunately, Marilyn transitioned while I was visiting her. I started making phone calls to tell people she had passed. In my silliness, even though Marilyn was lying there dead, I whispered on the phone in the room when giving the sad news. Why was I whispering? Marilyn had always thought I was a loud-spoken woman. Silly moments like that make me chuckle, and they ease the reality of challenging issues. I don't avoid pain, and I don't make light of issues, but I simply find comic relief or a rainbow in the storm.

Shortly after, God stirred the gift in me, and I started the training as a hospice volunteer. Over the years, God used me to give a hug, a smile, or comforting words to so many family members whose loved ones were in hospice. God allowed ongoing friendships because many of the surviving family members currently stay in contact with me.

Moving on Up!

Health problems upon health problems began to take a toll on me. Of course, the physical weight was a factor, as the doctors constantly reminded me, along with other ailments. Severe knee issues and a pinched nerve in my spine made it difficult for me to climb the stairs to get to my bedroom. I needed a place with everything on one floor.

One day, another dear friend Alta and I decided to go apartment shopping. We were both ready to sell our homes and reside in separate apartment suites where everything would be on one floor. Our first stop was a chic suburban apartment in Shaker Heights; the rental office itself was plush and had beautiful, soft carpet.

The leasing agent took us on a tour to see the model apartment. As we were mesmerized by the luxurious place, the theme song "Moving on Up" from the 1975 sitcom *The Jeffersons* was playing in my head. The agent asked if we'd like an application.

We both said, "Yes!" We were ready to get our own place since our children were all grown and had families of their own. *Will this be my new abode?*

After handing us the applications, the agent said the rent started at $850 per month for a one-bedroom. Two bedrooms, of course, would be higher, but we didn't bother to ask. We smiled and politely walked out of the apartment as if we needed time to think it over.

We kept our composure until we got in the car. Then Alta said, "I sure hope this old car starts so we can get away from this building and have a good laugh!" The car cranked up, Alta drove off, and by the time we passed in front of the beautiful building, we were laughing and mimicking the agent with her country dialect, "You can have a one-bedroom for $850, and we have two-bedrooms as well."

We both said, "She gave us an option for a two-bedroom!" We chuckled. "We cannot afford the one-bedroom!" We laughed all the way back to our inner-city neighborhood.

Over the years, God blessed me with good friends, but I think my best one was Maggie B. We had an awesome relationship. She and I were both from Mississippi and had migrated to Cleveland. Her husband and my sister's husband were brothers. To this day, my children refer to them as their uncle and aunt, and to their children as cousins. Maggie B. and I laughed and talked every day. We had a very tight bond, like sisters. We watched one another's children. We did house-to-house visits; her family would come to my home, or vice versa. The relationship changed somewhat when Fred and I left the family church, Charity Baptist Church, but the love was too deeply rooted for us to not stay in one another's lives. Although visits became few and far between, we were always there for one another! Maggie passed a few years ago, but she will always have a special place in my heart.

Another great friend of mine was Carrie. Carrie was dear to me. She was such a good friend. One day, I visited Carrie; her husband, Lee, was looking out the window on the second floor. Lee would not come down to speak that day, but after I went home, he came down to see if I'd left a sweet-potato pie. He asked Carrie, "Where is the pie?"

Carrie said, "Mae did not leave a pie!"

Lee said, "What she come over for?"

Carrie called me laughing and told me of Lee's disappointment when he did not see a pie on his kitchen table.

They were strong supporters of purchasing a pie anytime I sold them.

As time passed, Freda, my middle child, and her family were the only ones who lived with me. I shared with her and my son-in-law my need to move into a one-floor place because of a pinched nerve in my spine. They decided to purchase the home and relieve me of its responsibility.

My youngest daughter found a one-bedroom apartment in the suburbs of Richmond Heights, which was approximately thirteen miles from my Glenville home and from my neighbors on Pasadena, who were like family. The new place was freeway accessible, near my church, and centrally located for all my children. The rent was high at $500 per month for a one-bedroom, but I was going to make it work with my fixed income. Due to all my health challenges, I was no longer working, but I was receiving Social Security Disability Income.

I was never lonely because the children or grandchildren were constantly visiting. The grandchildren hung out with me practically every weekend.

Lord, Did You Bring Me Out Here to Die?

Four days after moving into my new apartment, I was in pain with kidney or gall stones. I drove myself to the doctor, and he did a procedure to burst them. I was able to drive myself home, and I was feeling fine. But once I got settled in bed, the pain was excruciating. I was so sick and afraid.

I cried out to God saying, "Lord, did you bring me out here to die?"

Lying in my bed, the Lord gave me a vision that appeared so real. I saw Reverend Pickett, the song leader and associate minister at Good Shepherd, lead the congregation in the hymn "Great Is Thy Faithfulness" at the old location of Good Shepherd on Shaw Avenue. "Morning by morning, new mercies I see."

I was sound asleep, but it was so real. I felt the presence of God and received healing. I said, "Yes, Lord, you did not bring me here to leave me!"

The pain ceased! God lifted that pain!!!! I was reminded of the Scripture, Hebrew 13:5, "I will never desert you, nor will I ever abandon you."

The lyrics of "Great Is Thy Faithfulness," the song that God gave me in the vision:

Great is Thy faithfulness
O God my Father
There is no shadow of turning with Thee
Thou changest not
Thy compassions they fail not
As Thou hast been
Thou forever will be

Great is Thy faithfulness
Great is Thy faithfulness
Morning by morning new mercies I see
And all I have needed Thy hand hath provided
Great is Thy faithfulness
Lord unto me

Pardon for sin
And a peace that endureth
Thine own dear presence to cheer
And to guide
Strength for today
and bright hope for tomorrow
Blessings all mine, with ten thousand beside

Great is Thy faithfulness
Great is Thy faithfulness
Morning by morning new mercies I see
And all I have needed Thy hand hath provided
Great is Thy faithfulness
Lord unto me

CHAPTER 11

Back to Reality

Well, reality was setting in. I needed a one-floor place that I could afford with my Social Security Disability Income. The apartment rent was increasing every year in Richmond Heights. I decided to search for low-income housing because of my disadvantaged income. There were a few options in Cleveland and the Cleveland Heights area, but all had a waiting list, except the Morning Star Towers on East 106th and St. Clair in the Glenville community.

Morning Star had a one-bedroom apartment with a balcony available on the second level. The place was so small, yet affordable. The kitchen, dining area, and living room were all in one room. The bedroom was a comfortable size and would accommodate my traditional bedroom set that included a queen-sized bed, rectangular dresser with mirror, and armoire. I moved in shortly after applying.

Initially, I loved Morning Star Towers. I had no shame returning to the inner city. You must be strong in who you are and whose you are—God's child—and know that life is a journey, even if it appears you are walking backwards. Now, I am back near my family and friends. I have friends residing in the building, and as a person who loves people, it was not hard to meet and acquire new friends.

Shortly after settling in my new, quaint home, I attended the annual, beautiful Christmas party in the multipurpose area of the building. Building management served us dinner, hired a DJ, and gave all the residents a gift in appreciation for being a tenant. The ladies got dolled up and put on our party dresses or pants suits, and the men wore traditional or walking suits.

As we stepped off the elevator on the main floor, to gather in the multipurpose room, one could feel the energy of excitement and fun as some good old Luther Vandross escaped from the party room. Yes, even we seniors enjoyed Luther and other good, clean rhythm-and-blues artists.

I was not a dancer, but I enjoyed watching others spin around on the dance floor and "cut a rug." Well, those seniors were not literally cutting anyone's rug, but they thought they still had the moves. I know Ben-Gay or some other type of liniment was calling them the next day, or maybe even that night. Oh, the fun they had showing off on the dance floor.

Those like me who did not dance had the room filled with laughter and great fellowship. This was the best medicine for us seniors. One of the guys—we will call him June Bug for laughs—I had met in the lobby earlier that year when I was completing the lease agreement for the apartment; he approached the table where I and others were seated. He greeted us and joined our group. He shared with the others while looking at me, "I be tryin' to get to Mabel, but she keeps her car filled with her grandchildren. I believe she got a hundred of them!"

All of us at the table laughed. As we were laughing hysterically, I reminisced about the day I met him in the lobby. As I was headed to the office to submit my lease agreement, he said, "Mabel, when are you going to invite me to your apartment for breakfast? I am invited to a different apartment every morning for breakfast."

I said, with my pretty Ms. Mabel smile and a chuckle, "You sho' as hell won't be coming to mine!" The other women in the building might be glad to have the male company, but I did not need it. Not after thirty-five-plus years!

I laugh now and still say, "After Fred, I did my time!"

June Bug and many other residents appreciated my candor and personality. You, the reader, may ask, "Mabel, what would Jesus say?"

Well, I have always been quick-witted and can come up with Jesus-like, beat-the-people-out-of-the-temple-style comebacks and laughs! I became friends with many of the men and women in the building because they all respected me for being forthright. They knew who I was and what I stood for. They knew that if they ever needed someone to talk to, I was going to direct them to Scripture. You can feel safe talking to me; there is never any judgment, but expect an honest, frank, and trustworthy response.

After the ones who loved to dance sweated out and became tired from dancing, the DJ transitioned from club-style to church-style music with the first song being "Amazing Grace," followed by other old-school-gospel vinyl records. I laughed in my spirit at the drastic change of not just the music, but also the people's demeanors—not in a bad way, just recognizing and referencing God. The Christmas party was an annual event that the residents looked forward to every year.

As mentioned, I love people, and it is in my DNA to serve them, especially the elderly. There was an elderly lady, Mrs. H, down the hall from me; she was unable to care for herself. One morning, she called me and frustratingly uttered, "Harrison, my home-care aide, cannot cook oatmeal!"

I assured her that she would be all right and that I would prepare a bowl of oatmeal for her. I enjoyed taking care of her when she called me from time to time.

One day, I was out taking my grandchildren to school and visiting my friends who were in the nursing home. During my absence, Mrs. H called the office manager in our building and asked for an ambulance to take her to the hospital so that she could be transferred into a nursing home. She expressed her various needs, including her inability to do her own laundry and prepare her three-square meals. She said, "Harrison comes over to help, but has too many responsibilities of her own to attempt to take care of me."

Later that day, I returned to my building; the lady who worked in the office saw me, stopped me, and told me that Mrs. H, my friend, had requested to be taken to the hospital for an evaluation and referral to a nursing home. She was at Indian Hills where she could get the proper care.

I immediately turned around and went straight up to the nursing home. Mrs. H did not have children, only a guardian. When she saw me, she smiled and said, "Baby, today was a rough day! I can't take care of myself. I appreciate all that you have done for me, but it is best for you and me that I reside in this nursing facility." After that, I visited her at least once a week so that she would not feel alone.

One year, my family had a Mother's Day Fundraiser Dinner in my building to support our Sharp Family Reunion Fundraiser. My niece Norma and I did the cooking, and a team of family members decorated the multipurpose room with beautiful tablecloths and centerpieces and served the people. I reached out to many residents for their support.

A few of the mothers in the building said with an uppity attitude, "Oh no, my children will be taking me to a nice restaurant for dinner." I encouraged them to enjoy their special day with the beautiful gesture from their children. Later, I would see them in line ordering one of our dinners. I did not question or comment, but politely told each of them, "Happy Mother's Day, enjoy your meal."

The room was filled with support from many. We even had men who would come just to get a good, old-fashioned, homemade meal. Also, many of the family members, who were not on one of the teams to cook, serve, or clean up, purchased meals to support the fundraiser and ensure we reached our goal.

As I became comfortable in my new place of residence and saw the success of the Christmas party and fundraiser, I reached out to the management of Morning Star Towers to inquire if I could organize monthly bazaars in the spacious multipurpose room. The manager and I agreed to rent tables for ten dollars each to whoever wanted to participate in selling their products, such as good, old-fashioned buttery-flavored baking goods, gently worn clothes, handbags, artwork, crafts, and other items. We placed notices in the mailbox of every tenant in the building and post flyers in the lobby, multipurpose room, each laundry room, and the elevators. All were asked to share the bazaar information with their family and friends so that we would have a range of people to whom to sell our goods.

I encouraged others in the building and family members to rent a table and sell their specialties. As an Avon representative, I sold my Avon products. I also purchased bulk items from the wholesale store and sold various items, such as soda pop, bottled water, Honey Buns, and Moon Pies. I enjoyed baking and selling my signature sweet-potato pies and peach cobblers. As a plus-size woman, I knew people of my size appreciated finding bargains for my gently worn clothes.

We participants sat in the multipurpose room and sold our items all day. The bazaar allowed people to come out of their small apartments and meet new people, fellowship with neighbors, and shop in the convenience of their building. I and the others had a wonderful time and made a little extra money to stretch our income, but the value of putting smiles on the tenants' faces was priceless. Many seniors do not get visits from their family, so to be able to connect with other people once a month was a blessing for many of them.

One Monday, after one of the weekend bazaars, a young lady knocked on my door. I had seen her in the building, but I was never good at remembering names, so I referred to her as darling or honey. Turns out, I was too friendly and gullible. I allowed her to come into my apartment and talk. I figured we could continue our previous conversations. She expressed so convincingly how much she appreciated me because I would share the gospel of Christ and was a great listener who provided a wealth of wisdom. I enjoyed providing *Our Daily Bread* devotionals to many of the residents on my floor and others whom I would encounter.

At the end of her visit, she asked if she could use the bathroom. Without any hesitation or concern, I immediately said yes. As she was walking to the bathroom, she must have spotted my purse in the bedroom, grabbed it, and taken it with her into the bathroom. She stole twenty dollars from it. Thank God, I did not have any of the money profited from the bazaar in my purse.

She came out of the bathroom, went to my balcony, and yelled to someone outside that she was on her way. When she left, I noticed my purse on the bathroom door and knew that I'd gotten scammed. Immediately, I reported the incident to the guard, but he pretended that he did not know her and had not seen anyone fitting the description I gave. No one in management or security supposedly knew anything about her.

She was the last person whom I allowed in my apartment. From that time forward, only family members or friends were allowed to enter. The experience rattled my nerves to the point that I was uncomfortable getting on the elevator since there was so much traffic and so many young people who made me feel fearful, such as unprofessional home-health-care providers and tenants' children and grandchildren.

Two of my dear friends who resided in the building had sons who were in and out of jail and would occasionally live with them. Their sons were so respectful. Rumor had it that they were stealing from residents in the building, but they never stole from me. They were so polite and always greeted me with a "Hello, Mrs. Harrison."

Time passed, and I was more cautious, watching my surroundings and putting the top chain lock on my apartment door. I refused, however, to allow fear to cripple me. I would walk the long hallway multiple times daily as a form of cardio workout.

One evening, I decided to walk the hallway, and on the last lap, I stopped in the laundry room to look out the window and check on my car to ensure that it was still how I left it. Unbeknownst to me, I walked right into a drug transaction. I gave a greeting, a smile, and pretended that I hadn't seen what was going on; I proceeded to peek out the window, turned to exit, and told the guys to have a good night. I quickly walked to my apartment and locked the door, putting the chain lock on as well.

I was so nervous at having personally witnessed drug activity that the next day I went down to the office to let them know I would be looking for a larger place. Seeing drugs in the building where I resided was the straw that broke the camel's back. For the younger readers, that means that was the last bad thing that I wanted to deal with where I lived. Out of fear, I did not report the drug activity to the people in the office, but I drove all day, looking for apartments, only to be placed on waiting lists.

Abington Arms Apartments—across from Case Western Reserve and a block from University Hospital, where I went for all my various doctors' appointments, including specialty doctors—really caught my eye because it appeared so gorgeous on the outside with meticulous landscaping, beautiful flowers, and an outdoor pavilion with picnic tables. It was exceptionally clean on the inside. I desired a two-bedroom so that my cousin Rosa Lee would be able to stay with me.

Trusting God to protect me until they had an opening and I could move, I got busy serving others to keep my mind off my current situation. I stayed on the go!

Every year while my granddaughter was attending Ohio University (OU) in Athens, Ohio, I was her guest for Parent/Grandparent Weekend. My oldest niece had two children attending OU as well, so she drove us down to the beautiful, traditional 1,800-acre campus on Thursday; we returned to Cleveland on Sunday. It was a little over a three-hour drive each way.

Ohio University was the first university chartered by an act of Congress and the first to be chartered in Ohio. The beautiful Alumni Gateway, also known as the Memorial Gateway, frames the entrance to this traditional college campus; it is engraved with a Latin inscription that translates to "So enter, that daily thou mayest grow in knowledge, wisdom, and love." What powerful words were carved into that stone decades ago, yet they were fitting for the particular weekend I was afforded the opportunity to sit and be showered by wisdom and love through the words of the beautiful poet Maya Angelou. She was the special guest for that Parent/Grandparent Weekend, and she shared so much wisdom, empowering the young and the old. We all left her presence feeling inspired to be a "rainbow in the clouds."

My granddaughter's friends adored me, making me feel special and loved, and made a fuss over whose grandmother I was. One of her friends was too silly, loved to drink; she teased and said, "Gramma and I are going to go party! Aren't we, Gramma?"

I said, "Not in this life!"

She chuckled and said, "Oh, Gramma, come on!"

My granddaughter said, "Gramma and I are putting a lock on the door to keep you out!"

My first Parent/Grandparent Weekend, four of the girls, including my granddaughter, lived in this spacious place, and the mother of one of the girls cooked. The two of us got in that kitchen and made delicious meals that weekend for the girls and their parents to enjoy! We had a blast!

The fourth and last year's Parent/Grandparent Weekend, my granddaughter and I got up and went out for breakfast without her friends and their parents. As she was driving, I saw a little store that grabbed my attention; it resembled a yard sale. I hollered out with joy and excitement, "Evalena, stop!"

She chuckled and did as she was told.

We walked in this little store, and I saw a white breakfast set for fifty dollars. That was my gift to Evalena for the four years of inviting me up to hang out with her and her friends and for her accomplishment of obtaining an undergraduate degree. I was so proud of her. She was the second of my children and grandchildren to earn a four-year college degree.

My granddaughter Sharene in Michigan was the first in the family to obtain a bachelor's degree. She received a bachelor of education. A few others have obtained their bachelor's and have gone back and completed their master's program. All my children and grandchildren may not have completed college, but all have made me proud of their work ethic and independence. The grandchildren are really tapping into entrepreneurship, walking in their passion and purpose. A degree is wonderful, but not necessary if you are walking in your purpose and complete the mission you were created to accomplish on this side!

CHAPTER 12

C'mon, Jesus!!!!

Well, I was finally approved for a sixth-floor, one-bedroom apartment in Abington Arms on Mayfield Road off Euclid Avenue. My daughter Freda suggested that I not rent the fourteenth-floor apartment that was originally offered. She said, in case the elevator went out or there was a fire, walking down that many flights of stairs may be too challenging due to my health issues.

The scheduled moving day was fast approaching. It was not God's will that my cousin share an apartment with me, but I was excited to be moving into a safer community. Lori and I went furniture shopping for my new home. She purchased a new flaxen-colored, floral-print couch that caught my eye, a solid forest-green chair for my living room, and a dining table with chairs that would go well with the Cherry Grove Breakfront China Cabinet that my oldest son, Ted, had purchased years prior when he refurnished my home on Pasadena.

All my children and grandchildren who lived locally helped me pack and move into my new place. I do not take for granted the team effort and support that my children provide. They are always there for me when I need them. As new furniture was arriving, my new place was becoming a home and giving me a fresh start to a new season in my senior life.

Initially, Abington Arms appeared to be modern, clean, and friendly. My original social worker in this senior-citizen building was phenomenal. She tended to my various needs and educated me on the many benefits and programs that I was eligible for as a senior citizen, such as my first RTA Card that would allow me to ride the public regional transportation for a huge discount. She informed me of a computer class that was provided for seniors in the building, to aid us in becoming familiar with the rapidly growing tech world.

Baptist to Nondenominational

There, I met a wonderful young man named Ron, who was the instructor. He was patient and kind with us seniors. He and I connected immediately, only to realize that we were members of the same church, New Community Bible Fellowship, where I was led to join after the passing of my dear friend Norma Hawkins, the first lady of my previous church and its rock and glue.

You will never find another like Norma Hawkins; she had a meek but firm way of keeping us strong, opinionated women grounded. She also had the people skills to hug and give a gracious smile to seemingly all the members. The first ladies of the church who succeeded her are both beautiful, godly women, but God was telling me that my season at Good Shepherd was ending. It was time to step out into a different style of worship.

New Community Bible Fellowship (NCBF) is a nondenominational church that was different from what I was accustomed to as a Baptist all my life. They did not use hymn books or multiple choirs, as in my previous churches. There was no big pulpit for the pastor and associate ministers to sit high and exalted above the congregation in a colonial style—high center chair and two side pulpit chairs made of high-quality wood, covered with solid-colored cloth, and thickly padded backs and seats for comfort. The first lady did not sit prominently in the front, wearing a stylish dress and matching hat so you would recognize her immediately as the pastor's wife.

The NCBF had a style that was far from deficient, but completely different. All the churches I had attended up to that point were some denomination of the Baptist Church, whether Southern Baptist or Fundamentalist Baptist. They all had a mother's board—a group of women, longtime members of the church, who assisted in the functioning and activities of the church—sitting in the front row of the church and dressed in white every first Sunday. I was accustomed to a Communion table—in front of the pulpit and bearing the inscription "Do *This in Remembrance of Me*"—and hand fans made with a wooden handle stapled to card stock that bore Martin Luther King Jr. or Mahalia Jackson's picture. But there was none of that at this church.

When I first attended New Community, I noticed that the stairs were steep and many to get to the level of the sanctuary. I looked at them and was determined to climb each one. The stairway, seemingly to heaven, was a task, so as time passed, I humbled myself and used the stair lift, even though I would visualize it malfunctioning, losing control, and throwing me down the steep incline at such a high speed I would continue right out the front door. I would laugh in my spirit and share my silly imagination with some of the greeters. They would chuckle, but always gave me the comical assurance that they would catch me.

The ushers were not in matching uniforms, but easily recognizable as greeters because of their warm, welcoming smiles and ready assistance on and off the lift. As the greeters at the entrance of the sanctuary provided me with a program that included sermon notes, they would escort me inside to a special section of seats for the seniors.

The service began with a few people on stage who sang praises and played worship music. There was no organ or piano, as in traditional churches, but drums, keyboard, various types of guitars, and sometimes a saxophone or violin.

As a woman in my eighties, do I miss some of the old-school hymns that brought me through tough times? Absolutely! Every now and then, the NCBF Minister of Music, Myron, would take us back to songs like "What a Friend We Have in Jesus" or "At the Cross." He sometimes assigned a soloist to sing songs like "Great is Thy Faithfulness." I adapted to the modern praises and worship music because I learned to pray in advance to prepare my heart and mind to receive the Sunday blessings that God had for me in the songs and the sermon.

At NCBF, the pastor sat in the congregation, on the front row along with other leaders, such as elders, ministers, deacons, and prayer warriors. He humbly rose and walked up the few steps on the side of the stage as he approached a small lectern to deliver his message. His sermons were outlined as a student from a seminary would do; they had a title, text that was a passage of Scripture, an introduction, three or four bullet points to help develop his message, and then a conclusion that challenged the audience to "a call to action." He might ask us to make a change moving forward in order to improve our Christian walk, or accept Jesus as Lord and Savior to begin the Christian journey. He was not an orator who gave you an emotional high or the conviction to "name it and claim it," but he was a solid teacher of God's Word to strengthen your walk as a believer in Christ.

The entire service never went beyond one hour and a half, and was typically shorter. I genuinely loved the humble innocence of my Pastor Kevin and First Lady Tanya, and the love you felt in NCBF. I had found my new church home.

Meet the Neighbors

One evening, I was getting my exercise by walking the halls in my apartment complex. My neighbor a few doors down had left her keys in the door. I politely knocked on her door and pointed to her keys with a smile. She was so upset with herself and thanked me with sincere gratitude. We introduced ourselves and became friends immediately. We started walking the halls together and talking each evening to make the time go quickly while getting our daily exercise.

Delores and I were friends up to her recent passing. Our favorite flower is the beautiful succulent plant, hens and chicks. We enjoy their beauty on our balconies during the summer and in our homes when we bring them in for the winter. We admire their low maintenance, not having to be repotted when transferred inside, and how easily they adapt to temperature changes.

As time went on, I met more ladies in the building who became dear to me, and our friendships remained strong as the years progressed. The relationships were forming even as some were dying of cancer, but they still appreciated my care and the meal or calming, encouraging words I provided.

Later, an ex-professional football player moved next door to me. He was tall, and his last name was ironically Long. He would keep his door cracked, seemingly just to use the noise of other people to keep from feeling alone. He admired my children and grandchildren who visited me regularly. He said, "Mae, you are blessed to have family." As he heard my children and the patter of my grandchildren's feet in the hall as they were coming or leaving, he would stop them and talk with them.

My gang knew he was lonely so they would accept his invite to sit in the living room and listen to his stories about his time in California as a professional football player with other celebrities. They were mesmerized by his experiences, but sad of his outcome. After all the fame, pretty women, and fast life, he'd ended up alone. They thoroughly enjoyed his company as much as he enjoyed theirs. When we would have family meals, one of the children would prepare a plate and carry it to him. He appreciated the unconditional love and care demonstrated by the family.

Time passed, and my social worker retired because she wanted to be a full-time grandmother and care for the needs of her grandchildren. I was given a new social worker, and that is when things began to change.

A few residents in the building did not care for the relationship that I had established with the original social worker. I shared with her the various fundraisers that I implemented at Morning Star Towers, which had been approved by management, and how those activities created a sense of community. I told her Abington Arms should consider bazaars and Christmas parties.

The social worker was so excited about my ideas that she shared them with the building manager and the residents who were overseers of community activities. They apparently were so afraid of losing their roles as leaders that they started giving me a hard time.

One day, a notice was placed in every resident's mailbox for an upcoming food bank where free food would be provided to all residents in the all-purpose area on the main floor. On the day of the food bank, I hopped on the elevator, got to the all-purpose area, and asked for the food.

A lady assistant asked, "Did you sign up?"

I politely told her that the notification I received said signing up was not necessary.

The main administrator spoke with a sharp and cutting tone, "Everyone has to sign up!"

I smiled and said, "No worries, darling! Have a blessed day."

As I was exiting, Peggy, who was in charge, looked at her friend and said something about "special privilege." I could not understand their attitudes. I had always looked at them as my equals. I never thought of myself as better, but I was comfortable in my own skin and knew who I was!

Another day, the manager in the building reached out to me and said that someone had called and complained about my balcony being cluttered and a big American flag hanging over the railing.

I asked the manager to please take a moment to look at my balcony and show me what the complaining tenant was referring to as an eyesore.

The building manager complied, saw a small, twelve-inch-round flag, and apologized for the misunderstanding.

I was never disrespectful, but as time went on, I realized that some of the other tenants simply did not care for me. I was fine with that. I was this new senior on the block who had a gift for smiling, bringing joy, and serving effortlessly.

I was living out my purpose that, unfortunately, possibly offended those who were unhappy with themselves.

I continued to be me with this attitude: "What people think of me is none of my business! It's not about them or me; it's about God!"

The C-Word

Time passed and around 1994 or 1995, I noticed that my energy was low, and I did not feel my vibrant self. I made a doctor's appointment with my primary care physician. He recommended testing and referred me to a specialist. I was scheduled for an MRI, magnetic resonance imaging, which involved my being placed in an uncomfortable, tight barrel. The findings—a tumor on my pancreas.

The doctor said, "Mae, with an aggressive cancer such as pancreatic, you will possibly have four to six months to live."

I was paralyzed and couldn't process this news. I thought if I ignored, it would go away. Finally, I spoke with the psychologist who had helped me cope with the passing of my son Freddie. She told me to tell my children. I said, "I am not telling the children nothing; they would go crazy."

In a subtle tone, she said, "Time is passing."

I went home and prayed; I gave God reasons why I should not die. One of the reasons was that all my children were married to supportive, hands-on partners, but Lori was still single at the time and did not have that kind of help with Lionel, her son. I then changed my prayer and said, "Lord, You got a thousand people who can help Lori raise her son. Your will be done." I went to sleep.

I woke up the next day and went into the bathroom to run my bathwater. My routine was to get up, run my bathwater, lie down because I was too weak, then get up, take my bath, and lie back down because I would be nauseated and weak. This morning, however, I easily took my bath, got dressed, and went into the kitchen to cook breakfast.

The phone rang, and it was a friend, Nina. She asked me how I was doing. I said, "I am fine." And that's when it hit me—I AM FINE! I AM WELL! I dropped the phone and shouted in my spirit, "I am fine!" I picked up the phone and said, "Oops, Nina, I dropped the phone trying to cook." We laughed and chatted.

I never told Nina what was really going on. I went to the doctor two weeks later, and it was confirmed; they could find no cancer. God is faithful! God is a healer!

God even provided Lori with a husband the following year. They had a small intimate wedding in my son-in-law's spacious backyard, with a harpist who played various melodies that put love and unity in the atmosphere. Her colors were a beautiful forest green, black, and white.

Trial after Trial!

Well, Kentucky Derby weekend of 1998, not that I am into horse racing—Lori's husband owned and raced horses, so that is how she remembers that weekend because she was the only one in town—Lori was at home, and she received a call from my granddaughter Sharene. I was out of town, so Lori had no way to reach me with the news she'd been given. Cell phones were not that popular for my family members, and especially for people my age on a fixed income.

I came home that Sunday after another Parent/Grandparent Weekend with Evalena. I entered my apartment, only to see my answering machine lit up with numerous messages. I listened to multiple Saturday messages from various family members; they all asked me to give them a call. I assumed that many were calling to say they were back in town or checking in to see if I made it back in town.

I called Lori, only to hear the upsetting news that Gwen, the oldest of my children, had died. The week before, I had visited Gwen in the hospital, but I did not know that God would take her so soon. Yes, she was having similar challenges to those of her dad, but she was our child. God would not take her from her young-adult children.

The week before, I remember telling Gwen while visiting her in the Detroit hospital that I would be back to make sure Sharene, her youngest daughter, had a wonderful graduation party.

She smiled and said, "Thanks, because I want her to feel like a queen! I am not going to make it out of the hospital alive."

I paid her words no mind! I said, "We got work to do in making sure the first graduate from a four-year college in our family is celebrated." I did not know that would be the last time I saw Gwen.

Hearing the unexpected news of her death was a bite in the stomach because I had every intention of being there to help Gwen, not just with the graduation party, but caring for her as she healed.

We all carpooled to Detroit for the services. Another moment for me to see that my children have formed a strong support system. Gwen's children went above and beyond in providing her with a beautiful Celebration of Life service. I was so proud of their strength and love that they expressed for their mother. During the service, a friend of my grandchildren sang "Mama" by Boyz II Men, and everyone was moved. They even had Marvin Winans sing a song. The entire service was special. I returned to Cleveland the next day after having breakfast with my grandbabies.

The following weekend, we all went back to Detroit to ensure that Sharene would feel love and support during this tough Mother's Day season as she marched across that stage to receive her bachelor's degree. We were so proud to witness this great accomplishment. As Sharene walked across the stage, she looked up and lifted her diploma to heaven, as if to say, "I love you, Mom. We did it!"

Our emotions were heavy, but as I had promised Gwen, the graduation party would have all the fixings. I followed through with the children's favorites, such as candied yams and all the delicious soul food. During this bittersweet weekend, we laughed and hid the tears to make it a joyful weekend.

As we returned to life, coping and pushing, days went by, and seasons were changing. Winter was approaching, and my mom was getting ready to get on a Greyhound Bus to celebrate her birthday that December. She was excited to be honored and celebrated.

My mom was comical. She was the type to receive a birthday card and shake it, waiting to see if money fell out, before thinking about reading it. We laughed each time we celebrated her special days and said, "Mom, you read the card?"

She would give us that innocent look of hers, smile, and with an "oh Jesus" chuckle, start reading the card.

Wednesday evening before getting on the bus, Mom called my sister and me to check in. She had packed and gotten her hair done. Mom was so excited. Yes, she was ready and did not mind getting on a Greyhound and riding that long distance, even at her age, with her older sister.

Later that evening, with no shower in her home, Mom got in the bathtub and bathed. Yes, Ms. Sadie Mae was ninety-one and was still able to sit in a bathtub. After putting on her night attire, she went into the living room and sat in her favorite chair to rest her eyes. She was a roadrunner, so if she ever slowed and sat down, a nap would happen immediately. Except this time, she did not awaken. She closed her eyes, only to transition to be in God's presence.

My brother Mozell, who had relocated back to Mississippi years prior, was Mom's rock; he called and told me she passed. The entire family was devastated. She was a vibrant woman, even at her precious age. She had just recently stopped driving, at my brother's insistence, but she was a self-sufficient person who took care of everyone!

Jesus, not again! As you know by now, I deal with pain by talking, eating, and staying busy. I kept people around me. I showed no emotions. My objective was to make sure everyone else was all right. My sister, her husband, and I flew, and all my children drove, down a few days later.

My oldest grandson, Richard, who had just buried his mom earlier that year, came from Detroit to be there for me. They all drove down a day or two before the funeral services and stayed in the motel a few miles down the road. I was happy to see my children and grandchildren from Cleveland; they were always there for me. But seeing Richard was even more special. What a selfless act. He hugged me, understanding and empathizing, while my children supported me and sympathized over losing my mom, their Big Mama. They loved their Big Mama, some on the same level as a second mom, but the loss of your actual mother is unexplainable. But tough Mabel had to be strong for everyone else.

We had a beautiful Southern Homegoing service for Mom. In fact, it was the traditional country ritual in which family members—for us, many of her grandsons—dug the grave early that morning before the service in the red-clay cemetery next to the church where my son Danny, my dad, my brother, and other loved ones were buried. Although there were tears during the funeral service, there was also a lot of laughter. As mentioned, my mom was a comedian, so many who spoke kind words reminisced about the funny moments. Many stayed a day or more after the service to simply fellowship and enjoy one another's company.

No matter life's challenges, God reminds me of his awesome strength.

Thy word have I hid in my heart
(Psalms 119:11, King James Version)

The Joy of the Lord is MY STRENGTH!
(Nehemiah 8:10)

God is MY REFUGE AND STRENGTH, an
ever-present help in trouble.
(Psalms 46:1)

The name of the Lord is a STRONG tower;
the righteous run into it and are safe.
(Proverbs 18:10, New King James Version)

If you are feeling weary, afraid, and weak, and need God's divine
touch, simply study Scriptures on God's strength. They will
remind you whom you can truly turn to for STRENGTH.

CHAPTER 13

I Must Tell Jesus

Sunday dinners fade, family gatherings fade, and holiday gatherings fade. Year after year, seemingly the close-knit family began to fade, but not completely disappear. Everyone wanted to create their own paths and new traditions, but I wish they were a little more considerate of the whole versus the part. I was hurt, but my pride said, "I do not mind eating alone." Many days, I felt like the structure of this apartment building. I was looking good on the outside, but there were so many challenges on the inside. I was losing my sense of purpose and living.

As we peel the layers of various challenges, which will be revealed throughout these next chapters, I kept my smile throughout and truly found joy in serving others as I continued visiting my friends who were sick and shut in the nursing homes.

Over the course of time, I had to have a hernia surgery. My daughter Freda has the gift of a nurse when it comes to caring for the disabled or sick. My other two daughters get easily squeamish at the sight of blood or the pouch that had to be changed. Freda came over regularly and changed the draining bags on my stomach.

Faith, her three-year-old daughter, saw my stomach and said, "Oooooh, Gramma has a long zipper." She had seen the clamps going from under my breast down to the hairline of my groin.

Freda and I just shook our heads and smiled.

Later, I had to face the challenge of knee surgery because the Motrin and Ibuprofen were not of any help, and the knee injection treatments were no longer an option for pain management. The doctor told me that I was dealing with severe osteoarthritis, meaning that between the bones there was a huge reduction of cartilage, which aids in the movement of the joint. I was now bone on bone. I needed or wanted to keep my independence and be able to walk and care for myself, not be confined to a bed or chair. I never wanted to be a burden to my children, so I decided to have the operation.

The day of the surgery arrived; the hospital waiting area was filled with my children and extended family members praying for me. My cousin Birdie, who worked at University Hospital in the operating rooms, told my children that, if I got through the anesthesia, I would be fine. The staff came out and provided updates after every stage, from sedation to procedure to recovery.

After the surgery, my children and other family members came to my bedside to spend some time with me. I was not feeling my best, so my extended family did not stay long. My children stayed longer as they watched me sleep most of the time.

The following day was when the hellion nurse was assigned to me. She treated me so badly. I recall lying in the bed and feeling dehydrated; my tongue was sticking to the roof of my mouth. I pressed the button to call the nurse for water and to tell her of the severe pain.

She bitterly explained that there were numerous other patients; I was not their only one.

One day, two of the former leaders of my church in the care ministry came to visit me. Before I could ring for help, a nurse was bouncing into my room and being extra polite to impress the two men from the church.

"Mae, is there anything you need?"

I smiled and said, "Yes, darling, some water, please."

When the nurse returned immediately with the water, I chuckled and sarcastically told the care ministry men to come back the next day to ensure I could at least get some water because the nurses had been unpleasant prior to their visit.

We laughed, talked about the goodness of God, and before they left, we prayed.

I have a high tolerance for pain, but this pain was excruciating, to the point that I thought I was going to die. It was time for me to go to my physical therapist to do the proper exercises to achieve the maximum range of motion and prevent stiffness, but the pain was unbearable. The therapist was sympathetic and pleaded with the nurse to provide pain medicine forty-five minutes prior to therapy. The merciless nurse would never provide the pain medicine in advance to give it time to kick in so that I would be somewhat able to do the rehab.

The day before my discharge, she admitted that she was having some issues with her daughter's rebellious behavior. She asked for my advice. Never take people's cruelty personally. The sayings are true. "People in pain give pain," and "Hurt people hurt people." Matthew 5:44 says, "Love your enemies; pray for those who persecute (hurt) you."

I was discharged from the hospital even though I was unable to do anything for myself. My therapist instructed me to move the knee as much as possible to avoid its stiffening. My children rotated shifts, providing my meals and bathing me. The pain was horrific!

One night, I was hurting so bad I cried out to God, "Dear God, You can do something about this." I knew this pain was not from God.

He heard my cry and gave me a reprieve.

During a follow-up visit with my doctor, I asked, "Why the long period of pain?"

He said, "Mae, physically you were not in pain."

I immediately responded defensively, "Oh yes! Most certainly! The pain was excruciating!" I shared with him my experience from day one of the surgery until recently when God removed the pain.

He kindly referred to my pain as psychosomatic, implying that the pain was psychologically driven. He explained that I had experienced something like chronic pain syndrome (CPS). Because of the severe pain that I experienced from day one, and as a result of not getting the proper medicine in a timely manner, it caused nerve fibers to send messages to my brain that said, "PAIN."

I was taken aback by the power of the brain. I thank God for His healing power and mercy because the knee replacement was the worst physical pain that I have ever experienced.

As time passed, I was back to my usual independent life. One day, I called my brother to check on him. He was fighting some health challenges. He was a natural comedian to the core; I think he missed his true calling. We laughed and talked, seeing who could bust each other's chops—tease in a playful way and outdo the other with jokes and silly fun. He was an ordained pastor as well, so we had conversations on what he was going to preach the next Sunday or what he would say on his small-town radio broadcast in Mississippi. I recall one of his favorite sermons that he preached was "These Dry Bones," taken from the text of Ezekiel 37.

Near the end of his life, we were on the phone, both trying to keep an upbeat, positive attitude. He said, "Mabel! I had a vision while lying in this hospital bed. The door opened, and there was a bright light telling me to come on! I said, 'You better close that damn door!'" We both laughed.

I said, "You are crazy! It may be a sign to get ready."

His comeback was "I made it right with God, but I am in no hurry to meet him now."

He was so much like my father. My children regard him as the funniest uncle.

It's My Birthday

My children and grandchildren came over to celebrate my birthday. It was not unusual for me to entertain a minimum of twelve people in my one-bedroom apartment. Although the tight, congested space agitated some, I was in my glory to have all my children, grandchildren, and some extended family around. There was no closet space to hang guests' coats or even a guest room to lay coats on the bed, as we would do back in the day. The grandchildren made my tight, crowded, fully furnished bedroom their dining area, using a portion of the bed for coat space when necessary.

The kitchen was standing room only for my girls to get a jump start washing dishes because I pulled out everything but the kitchen sink when cooking. I was never the clean-as-you-go type of cook because I was too focused on putting so much love in my cooking and ensuring that every dish was done with excellence.

During my birthday dinner, the loud laughter trickled into the hallway because of the door being slightly ajar to catch a breeze since the oven and stove caused the apartment to be quite warm, not to mention it was full to bursting with people. After my daughters cleaned the dining room table and kitchen and put everything away to create more space, we sat at the table to eat dessert.

The phone rang, only to hear the news that my brother Mozell had died. My sister and other family members came over as the news spread to loved ones. Although we were sad, we focused on memories that would make us laugh or smile.

Another Ruthless Nurse Testing My Christianity

Health challenges upon health challenges. Here I am, never smoked a day in my life, and I get diagnosed with COPD (chronic obstructive pulmonary disease), which is a lung disease that affects my breathing; it is caused by obstructed airflow from the lungs. After being admitted to the hospital, the doctor thought it would be best for me to go to a rehab facility and get the proper therapy to cope with my breathing. Ironically, my sister and I were both transferred within days of each other from the hospital to this gorgeous facility in the Richmond Heights area.

As I entered the facility, I saw so many patients and met them with a friendly hello and a heartfelt smile. God blessed me with a smile that invited many people to feel comfortable approaching me. He also gave me soft, kind words to minister to others about God's goodness. As I was getting comfortable in my temporary residence, I mingled with other patients. Many felt comfortable talking with me and relaxed, able to be themselves, whether they were White or Black. Sometimes people's emotional pain is so intense that they simply need a sounding board.

Residing in a nursing home indefinitely can cause a little anxiety for some people, especially those who do not have family support. I believe God used me to be a light for them, to encourage, to give hope, and for them to sense God's comfort.

Unfortunately, I had a nurse who was challenged by my unspeakable joy. Her odious behavior was exemplified whenever she came around. One day, a very pleasant nurse came to my room and provided extra bed covering. We exchanged pleasantries with laughter.

The discourteous nurse walked in, noticed the leg compression machine, and turned it off. She rudely said, "The machine is broken; you won't be able to use it today!"

The pleasant nurse gently and calmly said, "Mae, I guess we will have to improvise." She was the only nurse who would use the machine for my legs.

Whatever the other nurse was going through to be so mean was bigger than I was and bigger than the kind nurse who was helping me with grace.

Another day, I had occupational therapy and physical therapy, both twice. She came to my room to take me to therapy for the fifth time. I politely told her that I already had four therapies, and if I went to another one that day, it would come out of my pocket because my medical insurance would not pay. Neither physically nor financially could I afford a fifth therapy session.

Seemingly not listening to me, she said, in a very rude tone, "If you do not go to therapy, we can put you out!"

I said, "Oh, you do not have to; I will be happy to discharge myself! Bring me the papers!" By then it was 5:30 p.m., and I was waiting on dinner that was usually served at 5:00 p.m. I politely asked, "What time will I be receiving my dinner?"

In a sharp and abrupt manner, she said, "They will bring you your dinner!"

Although my sister enjoyed eating in the cafeteria, I refused to eat in there because of too many sickly patients coughing. As a germophobe in this setting, I preferred eating alone. Although at home I believed in having the table set for meals, I believed in clearing the table immediately after people ate. I simply did not like people breathing and talking over the food.

The next morning, I signed the discharge papers and went into the hall where I met the manager. I told him what happened.

He said, "Mae, you do not have to go."

I said, "It is time. I have been here for nineteen days." I could not afford to pay out of my pocket for additional care that my insurance did not cover, and I was unsatisfied with the treatment.

When you are often in the hospital, you will come across good nurses who seem sent from the Lord and others seemingly hellbound. I never knew her reason for being angry; it was not my business. Unfortunately, some people are agitated by a simple smile. This was another test for me to smile at Satan's rage. Keep smiling because God has the last word.

I Must Tell Jesus

Written by Elisha A. Hoffman

I must tell Jesus all of my trials,
I cannot bear these burdens alone;
In my distress He kindly will help me,
He ever loves and cares for His own.

> *Refrain:*
>
> *I must tell Jesus! I must tell Jesus!*
> *I cannot bear my burdens alone;*
> *I must tell Jesus! I must tell Jesus!*
> *Jesus can help me, Jesus alone.*

I must tell Jesus all of my troubles,
He is a kind, compassionate Friend;
If I but ask Him He will deliver,
Make of my troubles quickly an end.

Tempted and tried I need a great Savior,
One who can help my burdens to bear;
I must tell Jesus; I must tell Jesus:
He all my cares and sorrows will share.

What must I do when worldliness calls me?
What must I do when tempted to sin?
I must tell Jesus, and He will help me
Over the world the vict'ry to win.

CHAPTER 14

A Black President: These Aged Eyes Have Seen It All

On January 20, 2007, Hillary announced her candidacy for the presidency. Her husband, former President Bill Clinton was affectionately embraced and highly supported by the Black community. Toni Morrison, acclaimed novelist, eloquently described Bill Clinton the way many in our community viewed him; she said he was "Blacker than any actual Black person who could ever be elected in our children's lifetime. After all, Clinton displays almost every trope of Blackness: single-parent household, born poor, working-class, saxophone-playing, McDonald's-and-junk-food-loving boy from Arkansas." In fact, many supporters admired the Clintons and thought Hillary was the brains of that duo, so if she was considering the presidency, she could possibly get the support of many Blacks.

On February 10, 2007, three weeks later, the handsome young Senator from Chicago announced his candidacy for the presidency of the United States. Many of us thought that this Black man would not stand a chance against Hillary Clinton. Various questions gave doubt. Such as, was he too young? did he have enough experience? and was the country ready for a Black president? Although it was exciting to see a positive representation of the African American community running for president—a beautiful wife, rich melanin skin, full lips, beautiful cheek bones, curvy shape, hair texture like my daughters', and words, accents, or even gestures relatable to Blacks—is there a place at the table for us?

No matter the odds stacked against them, the Obamas persevered. They were gaining traction with their three infamous slogans—"Hope," "Change We Can Believe," and "Yes, We Can!" He had a lot of work to do to convince the older voters, but he was immediately heard and supported by the millennials. The college students, Black and White, were excited to see someone young and relatable.

I never thought I would see the day a Black man became president of the United States. Dr. Martin Luther King Jr.'s "I Have a Dream" speech dates back to August 1963. Is this our season for favor as African Americans? Would his dream come into fruition on this level?

I watched and tuned into the political channels as this young guy was gaining popularity. He was tall, elegant, and fresh. He was becoming popular like a rock star. What was his message? What was his vision? His speeches were filled with "together" and "let us" and closed with "God Bless the UNITED States of America!" He always emphasized the "united." His platform was empowering, not just for the Black community, but for all people to transform a nation. His words that were spoken profoundly gave hope for better schools, jobs, and health care for all. His vision empowered people to not fear, but to walk in our purpose. He was a great orator whose speeches were riveting, not only in the United States, but all over the world. He had been a professor for many years, teaching constitutional law, so that was certainly an advantage when his opponents tried to label him as "just a community organizer."

During his campaign, thousands of people were lining up to see him, no matter the weather at his campaign rallies.

When the crowd counters estimated 5,000 spectators, that number was exceeded by wide margins. There were crowds reportedly of over 100,000 people who just wanted to witness with their own eyes a Black man running for president of the United States of America. Overall, the rallies were very peaceful, but the "mama" in me prayed for his safety and the well-being of him and his entire family.

The energy in the crowds was electrifying, according to my daughter Lori and grandson Lionel, who attended at least two of his rallies. They spoke candidly of the experience, including how the crowd would boo the current Bush administration, and how politely, but firmly, Barack Obama would say, "Don't boo! GO VOTE!"

His profound speeches at the rallies energized his base for early voting. My daughter Lori and I went to the Board of Elections and stood in the long line. The excitement was real; people openly and candidly expressed their love for Barack Obama. Many were hoping for change, no matter if you were Democrat, Republican, or Independent.

November 4, 2008, the results were trickling in as each state projected the electoral-college votes. After the experience with President George W. Bush and Vice President Al Gore during the 2000 presidential election—Al Gore won the popular vote by more than 500,000, but George Bush won the electoral college vote 271–266—many focused on what matters, and that is your candidate reaching 270 electoral votes.

Around 11:00 p.m. on the East Coast, the networks were making the historic announcement of the first African American chief executive of the United States. A few family members called me in disbelief yet joyful, wanting to know my true feelings at seeing history of this magnitude.

As a person who grew up in a segregated South, I never thought that I would see this day. I believe John Lewis said it best that night in an interview on MSNBC, and I'm paraphrasing here: It was "unbelievable to see a young African American man as President of the United States. We are a better nation and prepared to come together, laying down our dark past."

As I looked at the massive diverse crowd at Grant Park in President-Elect Obama's home city, awaiting his appearance, I watched the tears flow from Reverend Jesse Jackson's eyes and Oprah's arm rest on the shoulder of a White man. People of every ethnicity were united, crying, cheering, and celebrating this historic night. Then the announcer said, "Ladies and gentlemen, the next First Family of the United States."

This beautiful family walked onto the stage, color-coordinated in their beautiful red and black attire, as the crowd roared. This family looked like me and my family. What a beautiful sight to see! They waved to the crowd, displaying humility, love, and gratitude. Michelle and the girls disappeared from the stage after the president-elect gave each one of them a kiss and a hug, showing a real-life version of the Huxtables from the sitcom *The Cosby Show*, which had displayed a positive image of a Black family.

Preside-Elect Obama approached the podium to begin his victory speech, and he remarked that "change has come to America." He started his speech with a shout-out to his hometown, Chicago, and then said, "If there is anyone out there who still doubts that America is a place where all things are possible, who still wonders if the dream of our founders is alive in our time, who still questions the power of our democracy, tonight is your answer." As the crowd cheered, he continued, "It's the answer told by lines that stretched around schools and churches in numbers this nation has never seen, by people who waited three hours and four hours, many for the very first time in their lives, because they believed that this time must be different, that their voices could be that difference. It's the answer spoken by young and old, rich and poor, Democrat and Republican, Black, White, Latino, Asian, Native American, gay, straight, disabled, and not disabled—Americans who sent a message to the world that we have never been a collection of red states and blue states. We are, and always will be, the United States of America."

What a great orator. I was moved by his victory speech and the days to follow.

Inauguration Day

January 20, 2009, in the blistering cold, with a windchill in the midteens and a high of twenty-eight degrees Fahrenheit in Washington DC, over two million people witnessed the inauguration of the forty-fourth president, Barack Obama.

I watched the inauguration of Barack Obama with Black cultural pride. A highlight for me were witnessing President-Elect Obama embracing John Lewis on the steps of the US Capitol moments from being sworn in as the next president. That took me back to the 1960s during the Civil Rights Movement. John Lewis had been devoted to equality since that era. He was the epitome of his famous saying, "Get in good trouble, necessary trouble." He was a man of courage, dignity, and honor. As a public servant, he had made so many sacrifices that almost cost him his life. The hug signified to me a big thank-you for all Congressman John Lewis had fought for over the decades, an affirmation that Congressman Lewis's labors had not been in vain. I implore young people to read the history of John Lewis to understand Black history and how far we have come. Although, there is still so much work to be done.

Another highlight was the infamous headwear adorning the Queen of Soul Aretha Franklin. As she approached the podium to sing "My Country, 'Tis of Thee," all I could say was "Sistah is wearing that hat"! Aretha took me to church with her soulful voice and gorgeous church hat. The hat had a grey, giant bow with sparkly, customized Swarovski crystals that grabbed the attention of many viewers. That beautiful hat was a conversation piece long after the ceremony. Sales shot through the roof for the flashy hat that Aretha purchased in Detroit, Michigan, for approximately $179.

Some people of other ethnicities could not relate, but if you were a Black woman of my era, you would have an appreciation of such style. A hat symbolizes a woman's crown in the Black church. The older women take pride in fashionable, stylish hats. I have always loved a stylish hat adorned with ribbons, bows, or even a feather.

There were so many moments, such as seeing Obama's beautiful wife and daughters, that filled me with pride as an African American, but the highlight of it all was hearing this great orator give his inaugural address. In his address he said, "This is the meaning of our liberty and our creed, why men and women and children of every race and every faith can join in celebration across this magnificent mall, and why a man, whose father less than sixty years ago might not have been served in a local restaurant, can now stand before you to take a most sacred oath."

The crowd cheered, and Congressman Lewis stood and applauded.

I was in the comfort of my living room, cheering and saying, "YES!"

Obama then concluded his speech with quotes from George Washington and Thomas Paine. "In the face of our common dangers, in this winter of our hardship, let us remember these timeless words. With hope and virtue, let us brave once more the icy currents and endure what storms may come. Let it be said by our children's children that when we were tested, we refused to let this journey end, that we did not turn back nor did we falter, and with eyes fixed on the horizon and God's grace upon us, we carried forth that great gift of freedom and delivered it safely to future generations." He closed by simply saying, "Thank you. God bless you. And God bless the United States of America."

I was proud of Barack. He knew how to get his words across to the people. No free rides, no shortcuts, but all citizens working together and everyone doing their part, whether holding members of the US Congress and Senate accountable or voting at every election. I thought he was going to turn the world upside down in correcting the unfairness for minorities. I thought Blacks' opinions would finally matter.

Unfortunately, many of the people who voted him in did not do enough to make his vision a reality. Senator Mitch McConnell and the GOP were determined to make Obama a one-term president, and they filibustered any legislation that would help the middle class. I realize Obama is not God, and he is only one man! I was glad to see him reelected in 2012, but, again, many of his bills were opposed.

Going back and reflecting on the 2009 inauguration—I watched the parade, and each time the motorcade stopped and the Obamas stepped out of the armored limo to greet the crowd and walk a few blocks, my heart pitter-pattered. I began to pray, "Lord, protect the Obamas!" The crowd roared as they waved and smiled.

Also, I watched some of the inaugural balls, and the highlight of the Neighborhood Inaugural Ball was Beyonce's song "At Last," which she sang with grace and beauty. There were ten inaugural balls that evening. I could not hang with them the entire day, but some of the channels captured and replayed the coverage for days.

Over the years, during President Barack Obama's time campaigning and in office, I watched him give victory speeches, State of the Union addresses, campaign speeches, and many others, but the historic speech on racism, "A More Perfect Union," which many people believe was the game changer that saved his presidential campaign, was one of my favorites.

No Republican, Democrat, or Independent could fail to see history in the making as we watched this beautiful African American family become the United States of America's First Family. As a representation of the Black community, they succeeded on all levels in displaying unity, integrity, intelligence, education, and relatable, genuine love.

I wanted him to go down in history as a president of high regard, their children to have no negative images, and Michelle to not be stereotyped as the angry Black woman. Mission accomplished. God bless, they succeeded in keeping their strong positive image as they remained standing through the test of times.

To quote Michelle Obama's famous catchphrase, "When they go low, we go high."

Chapter 15

Lord, Deliver Me

One night in my apartment, something started buzzing in my ear. *Oh Lord, what if it is a roach?* I jumped up, tilted to the side for it to come out, but no luck. I got dressed, got in my car at 2:00 a.m., and drove to the University Hospital in Richmond Heights. I was too embarrassed to go to the hospital next to me. I did not want my doctors to know that the building where I resided might be infested with roaches.

Unfortunately, the Richmond Heights hospital did not have the proper tools or a doctor who could remove it, but they sprayed the roach to kill it. They advised me to go to University Hospital's main campus and see an ENT, an ear, nose, and throat specialist.

Later that day, I swallowed my pride, and the specialist removed it in ten minutes. The suffering I went through could have been easily avoided if I would have gone directly to the main campus, but my pride got the best of me.

As I returned to my apartment, I immediately went to the building manager's office and informed them of my situation. They told me that I would be added to the list, and it would be about two or three days. I refused to wait for management to address the problem. I was so embarrassed that I scrubbed my cabinets with bleach water and sprayed the entrance with roach spray. I mopped the entire place with soapy water, kerosene, and bleach—do not try this.

Living alone has its pros and cons. I like feeling useful and needed, so to keep myself busy, I involved myself in the caring for some of my grandchildren and in going to hospitals and nursing homes to see the sick and shut-ins. Also, I occupied my time on the phone, encouraging people at their wits' end with life. Whether the person was overwhelmed by health challenges or had issues with their marriage, finances, children, or loss of a loved one, I wanted them to refocus on their peace in the storm. God prepared me and provided a sound answer from His Word when I received those type of calls, or I would pray my way through the conversation. As I allowed the person to vent, at times I could relate and share my life experiences; we would always invoke the Word of God and end the conversation in prayer.

All of us are human, so our emotions become involved, and we can quickly feel overwhelmed by the burdens of life, but the Word of God is always comforting and soothing for the soul.

No More Driving

One day, I got in my car to drive to my primary physician, whose office was in Richmond Heights. As I was driving on the freeway, I noticed my exit. I started to slow down and get in the right lane. As I was coming off the ramp, trying to brake to slow down, my foot would not move off the gas pedal. It felt very heavy, like lead. I said, "Lord, protect me and others from an accident. If you get me safely home after my appointment, I will not drive again."

I was able to lift my foot and press the brakes to stop. Thank God, no one was in front of me, and no one was behind me, pressuring me to drive. I made it to my appointment, only to be diagnosed with other health ailments, such as neuropathy and fibromyalgia, to add to my preexisting conditions.

After my doctor's appointment, I went back on the Shoreway to get home, not thinking until I got off at my exit of the freeway that I would have been safer driving through the city. Again, God protected me, and I made it home and parked that car in Abington Arms' parking lot, never to drive again.

I shared what happened with my children and told them that it was time for me to let go of my steel-blue Caravan that my grandson Richard in Detroit, who owns a car dealership, had found for me. My daughter Freda and her husband had a friend who needed a car immediately, so I sold it to them. Although I would renew my driver's license until I was eighty-three, I gave up driving and never looked back.

Time to Move

In 2008, I desired a two-bedroom and asked my children to be on the lookout for me a larger apartment based on my income. The apartment was closing in on me; I cannot explain why, but there was a darkness or gloom that was overshadowing my place. I prayed, asking God for deliverance.

Four years passed. Management had set up an appointment for me to have new carpet installed in my place. I was glad to get new earth-tone beige-colored carpet; I figured it would bring some light and add a fresh touch to the apartment. Aww, the new smell of carpet. Later that night, I went to bed, only to awaken the next day to see my arms covered with fluid-filled blisters.

My neighbor's daughter drove me to the hospital, and the doctor said I was allergic to the pool water at the YMCA. Another day went by, only to have what looked like mosquito bites on my arms. I went to the emergency room for the second time, only to get the same result; I was again told it was possibly an allergic reaction. My granddaughter Reesie took me back home.

I was not using a different detergent; I had been loyal to Tide laundry detergent and Dawn dish detergent most of my adult life. The breakouts with itching would not go away; I was so aggravated and frustrated. My daughter Lori drove me to the emergency room for the third time to get to the bottom of this concern.

A younger doctor walked by, stepped into the door of the room as I was getting examined, and said, "Bed bugs!!!!"

I wanted to walk into the hall and whup him. I was embarrassed and upset, all at the same time.

Immediately when I got home, I called the manager in the building and told her my apartment had bed bugs.

She said, "Oh, that is impossible."

Ironically, my friend from the seventh floor called and said, "Mae, I am hearing a lot of complaints that there are bed bugs in that new carpet."

I called my son immediately and had him bring me some kerosene. I lightly dampened a mop with kerosene, went over all the carpet, and placed cups filled with kerosene under the bed. Please do not try this—according to the World Health Organization, ingestion of kerosene is harmful or fatal. However, after using this Southern remedy from decades ago, I never saw another bed bug.

I noticed a couple of residents on my floor getting their apartments treated. One resident had their mattress in the hall; it was being placed in a special cover. I found out later that cover was pesticide-impregnated to kill bed bugs. Once I shared my situation, other residents started being honest. They—even the neighbor whose daughter took me to the emergency room the first time—had bed bugs as well.

One day, I was in the hallway and noticed a man assisting an elderly lady who had an oxygen tank. She said, "It is cloudy." It seemed she was not getting oxygen.

In a very nasty tone, the man said, "I guess it is cloudy. LOOK!" There were roaches all through the oxygen-supply tubing.

I think I upset management when I said that I called the health department and other agencies to see what could be done. I would send management letters, only to receive responses that downplayed the issues in the building, possibly to avoid the building being closed. When you do not get along with management, and they try to downplay your concerns or nitpick, it is time to move!

The New House

Spring 2012, my daughter and son-in-law were looking on the Internet to acquire information regarding the vacant house across the street from them. They discovered that the home was on the Cuyahoga County Foreclosure Auction list, meaning it was a forced sale, and depending on how the bidding went, the price could be significantly lower than it would be through a realtor. But you are taking a risk; you are buying it blindly because you're unable to go inside the house to do an internal inspection and search for possible damage, such as electrical issues or water damage.

My daughter and son-in-law thought the minimum bid was affordable, so they made a bid on the house. They had the highest bid, but for whatever reason, the house was removed from the foreclosure sale.

A couple of months went by, and no one moved in; the house was still vacant. They went back online to see if maybe it had gone back on the auction block. To their surprise, not only was it back on the site for sale, but at a substantially lower cost. Again, they made the minimum bid, but did not realize the blessing that was in store.

See the power of God—they were the only bidders. They were notified that the bidding for that home was closed, and my daughter most likely, after lender approval and closing, would be its homeowner. They both, with doubting-Thomas spirits, said, "No way!"

They had their friend, who was a real estate agent, review the documents, and they were told the "paperwork looks legit." They still were doubting God's favor, so they had a lawyer review the documents. The lawyer said, "It is all legit; proceed with payment in full."

As new owners, they walked through the home and found no major work was needed except carpet and paint. The kitchen cabins were nice, electrical work looked new, roofing looked great, and foundation was sturdy. Excited, my daughter called me, told me of the blessing, and asked if she could come get me to look at it.

I said, "Sure, I am not doing anything."

As we pulled in the driveway, I said, "A brick home. Girl, that's a plus for you all, right there." We walked into the home through the side door. The kitchen was spacious; I said, "This is nice." We walked in the dining room that had nice hardwood floors. I said, "This is nice." On one side of the dining room was an office with a large window with a huge view of the backyard. I was in awe of the space. We walked through the place and looking into the living room, and I got a glimpse of my daughter's home across the road as I looked out the window. We walked farther down a hallway to see two bedrooms and a bathroom. I said, "Wow, this is nice!" We did not go upstairs because there were too many steps, but we did go view the finished, spacious basement that had a half bathroom. I was as excited as my daughter and told her, "What a blessing!"

My daughter looked at me and said, "Mom, do you want it? You said you wanted a two-bedroom. Here it is! Hubby and I were talking and believe it would be a headache to have tenants, so would you like to live here? The house is paid for; you can get the senior-citizen residential discount program for your utilities, and then your expenses should be equivalent to your rent at the apartment."

I loved the house; it was what I'd prayed for regarding space—two bedrooms, a larger kitchen, and a huge, gorgeous backyard, but I did not want to be a burden. I did not want it to become a financial burden; they would have to pay the property taxes and home repairs that I could not afford on my fixed income. I did not want her to ignore her own financial obligations and priorities to take care of mine.

I said, "Let me pray about it."

I went home excited for my daughter and called my son and grandson Lionel, talking about the beauty of the home. Later, I prayed, "Lord, what shall I do? I do not want to be a burden! I do not want them to feel obligated to fulfill my desire. Would this become costly for them? Lord, give me an answer." Later that night, I went to bed. As I lay down to sleep, God gave me a song in the night by Andraé Crouch and Marvin Winans, "Let the Church Say Amen."

A peace that I can't explain surrounded me.

The next day, I awakened with that same peace! I did my morning rituals of prayer, devotional reading, shower, taking my vitals, blood pressure and sugar tests, then breakfast. I called my daughter while eating, and I said, "I will accept the house as a gift. God has spoken. Let the church say amen." We both chuckled.

She said with joy, "Well, amen. Give me a few months to get it painted for you and wall-to-wall carpet installed so that you are not on a cold wooden floor, and allow us to get it senior friendly with grab bars, rails, and other necessary items to make it a safe and secure home. We will plan for you to move in by September 30. You are not allowed to see it again until move-in day." She asked me, "What do you desire to make this home to your liking?"

I said, "Eggshell color for the walls and rails at all stairs." I also told her I wanted to purchase my own appliances, so in August she took me shopping for a stove, a refrigerator, and a washer-and-dryer set.

As I made my selections, she asked, "Why are you purchasing all white appliances?"

I told her, "After my experience with the bugs, I want white everything to be able to see anything crawling. If anything moves, I will be able to see it." She shook her head, and we laughed.

As contractors completed painting the house from top to bottom and the carpet was installed on all three levels, all my children came together to clean the new place and pack up all my possessions at my old place. The support was overwhelming. Family and friends donated their time and energy; one dear friend provided money toward the new carpet. My nephew Michael added a concrete step and a security door at the side entrance. My son-in-law Tommy—his uncle is like a brother-in-law to me—installed grab bars in the shower and a handheld showerhead. An aluminum outdoor railing on the front steps was added. A dear deacon, Tyrone, from the church painted the trim on the house, and my nephew Henry worked on the garage. There was so much love given to make the move-in day more than I could have ever imagined.

My daughter envisioned a Harrison version of the old hit show *Extreme Makeover: Home Edition*. She wanted the street full of people to welcome me into my new home. We mailed and passed out invitations to all my friends and many of my children's friends.

Meanwhile, I gave management in my apartment building the proper thirty-days' notice that I was leaving. I shared with my closest neighbors that one of my children purchased a home for me and that September would be my last month residing in Abington Arms. Word traveled throughout the building that I was moving; there were random knocks at my door from residents, expressing their appreciation of my kindness as a neighbor and giving their blessings.

My neighbor Mr. Long came to my door and cried. He said, "You got family who genuinely love you, to get you out of this place, but the rest of us will die here." He loved my family and the support the children and grandchildren provided me.

The Saturday before moving, my children emptied my apartment out, washed everything down, and vacuumed the carpet, leaving everything clean. My daughter Freda took me to a real nice hotel in Beachwood to stay for the night before the big move-in day that they'd entitled "Move that Bus!"

Finally, the afternoon arrived, and Freda picked me up for the big celebration of my new home. As we drove down the street, there were many cars. I said, "No way, all these cars could not be for me."

As we got closer, I noticed a police car parked. There were so many people on the block that the mayor of the city thought, for safety reasons, a police car should be present.

My daughter dropped me off in front of the house. It was wrapped with a huge red-velvet ribbon with a bow on the front. Ted and Lionel escorted me to a chair next to my sister on the front lawn to enjoy the mini program before the cutting of the ribbon to view the house. I was flabbergasted by the mass of people who came to witness this special day for me. My neighbors provided chairs for some of the elderly guests.

My grandson who resides in Detroit has a recreational vehicle (RV) and was running late, so the emcee told the crowd to pretend the RV was present and say, "Bus driver, move that bus."

The people shouted out simultaneously, "Bus driver, move that bus"!

The program was led by Minister Myron, and the praise-and-worship team sang. My niece Sandy, who is in the choir back in Detroit, joined them and seemed a natural, as if this were not her first appearance with them. The beautiful songs echoed on the street. My heart was filled with joy.

Then out of nowhere, they sang Andraé Crouch's "Let the Church Say Amen." Let me remind you that this is the song that God gave me to confirm I needed to accept the home as a gift. Oh, honey, I was beaming with radiance. God is amazing.

After the singing, Maria, a prayer warrior at the church, prayed a blessing over the house and me. A few of my children and grandchildren, Nevin, Ted, Theresa, Lionel, and Lori, spoke kind words of me and why I deserved the home. Their words were so from the heart and moving that at times some would shed a few tears. One of my play-adopted children, Milton, said a few words about our friendship and then prayed his blessing for the house and me.

They asked me to stand to cut the ribbon.

"Do we have to cut it? Can't we save this beautiful big bow made by Lori's friend Danielle?"

The mayor of the city walked up the steps with me and gave me the scissors. Once I cut it, the long velvet ribbons hung down on each side of the porch. He then gave me a small box that had the key to my new home.

April, my granddaughter, opened the door, and we walked into the living room. My furniture from my apartment was placed perfectly; it looked natural and as if it belonged. I glanced on the wall above the couch to see one of my favorite Scriptures as wall art. It was taken from Ephesians 3:20: "God is able to do exceedingly, abundantly, above all we ask or think."

I never imagined the transformation of this house would be done with so much care and love on this magnitude. There were beautiful window treatments in every room. The sun porch had become an office with a desk and a bookcase. They even had the guest room furnished with a queen-sized bed with a beautiful comforter bed set. My bedroom had the furniture perfectly in place with a new, beautiful comforter bed set to match the window treatment. My white stove and refrigerator looked good in the kitchen. Freda had family pictures of my husband, children, grandchildren, siblings, parents, and cousins placed in black frames and hung on various walls throughout the house, looking as if I'd lived there for some time. My sister Fannie, Milton the mayor, and I were in awe of the love that went into every room. There was a color scheme in each room with at least one new item donated by my children and grandchildren. The Dunmore Cream—a neutral color—carpet throughout the entire house felt so good under my feet. I could not thank my children enough for all the hard work put into my home. All the boxes were unpacked.

The crowd had already dispersed by the time I went outside to thank the many people for coming out to share this special day. Lori had already advised them to please return another day due to limited space; I was expecting a busload of my grandbabies from Detroit. As I was standing out there, the long RV pulled up in front of my house. My grandchildren arrived safely. All of my babies were here to celebrate this joyful day.

The mayor blessed me and left. He was proud to see a beautiful, positive act done in his community.

The children served dinner, and we laughed and fellowshipped until nightfall. Home sweet home.

CHAPTER 16

God Still Answers Prayers

What a day! What a day! As I awakened in my new home, reminiscing about the day before and looking around at my new place, I could only say, "Thank you, Jesus!" I was jumping up and down on the inside. I slept so peacefully. No fear of being alone, but excited to be by myself for the first time in all my life.

I do not consider apartment living as being alone, especially in a senior-citizen building, because of the high traffic of people. There were too many people who would congregate in the lobby, seeing when you came and went. Also, whenever I cooked, the smell would ooze into the hallway. On many occasions, someone would knock on my door asking, "Mae, what are you cooking in there that has the hallway smelling so good?"

This beautiful morning, in my new home with a spirit of gratitude, I opened all the blinds, allowing all the light to enter because my other place only had two areas for sunlight to enter. This home was surrounded by windows. As I opened the blinds in my office, allowing the sunshine to seep in, I looked out into my beautiful huge backyard, imagining having a vegetable garden. But what did my wandering eyes notice? Oh Lord, Bambi...then another baby deer...then Mama deer.

I prepared my breakfast and sat at the dining room table listening to my favorite Christian radio station, WCRF—Moody

Bible. I ate and enjoyed my first breakfast, which included my favorites: oatmeal, Eckrich sausage, and a cup of coffee with two packages of Splenda and plenty of cream.

This new season was special. I could open the door, and no one asked what I was cooking. I was enjoying being alone and having my private space.

I am feeling grown-grown, sho nuff!

Many people who had a house did not understand why I wanted to move out of an apartment at my age and back into a home. My daughter even told me to look at the pros and cons of apartment living—the ability to interact with folks versus being alone in a single-dwelling home.

Although it provides privacy, will I get lonely?

God has seasons in our lives for various living arrangements, and for this chapter in my life, I appreciated the quiet.

One day, I noticed my daughter cutting the grass in the backyard. I said to myself, *I can get my exercise while she is out there doing yard work.*

As I walked in the backyard, I noticed the open area that did not provide any privacy between my neighbor and my yard. I told my daughter, "We are going to have to do something about this. I want complete privacy." I did not want to be concerned about teenagers running through my backyard.

I was able to hire a company to put me up a tall, eight-foot-high wooden fence before my first winter there. My house was becoming a home.

Spring arrived. My daughter Lori drove me to a few places to purchase some flowers. I love colorful annuals, such as different-colored geraniums, verbenas, marigolds, and zinnias, to name a few, with a spike to add as an accent in the center of the flowerpots. I intended to line the fence in the backyard with red or black mulch under those pots.

The two flower beds in the front of the house were covered with mulch and multiple flowerpots with my colorful flowers. My porch displayed my large ceramic flowerpots with a beautiful array of flowers with a rectangle flowerpot for my beautiful hens-and-chicks flowers.

This became our annual Memorial Weekend tradition—getting the yard beautiful to enjoy for the summer. I am in my glory when I am cooking or planting in the dirt. Lori enjoyed cutting the grass, taking pride in the diagonal lines that were noticeable on the plush bed of grass in the front yard, which her husband, Nevin, treated with fertilizer and grass seed to maintain a healthy rich-green, weed-free yard.

My first birthday was coming up. I decided not to do anything but relax and get mentally ready for the knee surgery scheduled the day after. My children came through to wish me well on the surgery and drop off birthday gifts. Yes, it was time for a knee replacement on the other knee.

God gave me favor on this second knee operation. The surgery and rehabilitation were much more tolerable than the first one. I decided to celebrate with a three-in-one bash. I was thankful to God to be able to celebrate another year of living, so the party was for my birthday, a successful knee replacement, and a year in my new home.

Labor Day brought sales on outdoor furniture. Sears, a department store, had good-quality chairs and tables at a discount price. I purchased umbrellas, tables, and chairs to host a backyard celebration at the end of September. I wanted my yard filled with people so that I could testify to the goodness of God.

We had such an incredible time that we decided to celebrate my birthday in the backyard every other year and at Cracker Barrel the opposing year. The biannual outdoor parties in June, with over one hundred guests, brought so much fulfillment in seeing my family and friends enjoy the fun, food, and fellowship. As I walked through the yard, hearing the plastic utensils scrape across the paper plates and people say, "Mae Bell, everything is delicious, and you put your foot in these yams," it gave me a profound sense of satisfaction. A spirit to serve is deep in my DNA. My mother enjoyed serving her family, which included her siblings, their families, those who were less fortunate than she, and the sick.

The yard was full of joy and laughter. My friend from Pasadena said, "Nobody gives a party like Mae." Another friend approached me saying, "Who has this many friends? Did you pay these people to come to your party?" Another friend set up her missionary table in the yard to educate us on her ministry in Africa; she told us how a small donation could bless a woman to receive personal hygiene products that were not available in some of the places where she missioned. My friends enjoyed the clean fun, with no alcohol or drugs permitted, and being a part of a mixed crowd of young, middle-aged, and more seasoned people interacting with one another with respect.

The younger people served the elderly their meals to avoid their standing for a long time in the line. The buffet tables were lined with our traditional spareribs, grilled chicken, fried chicken, candied yams, green beans, macaroni and cheese, potato salad, and dinner rolls, all in chafer dishes to keep the food warm; the potato salad was kept cold on ice.

There was a barrel with a variety of soda pops and bottled water.

Although the gifts were nice and in abundance, the greatest gift was seeing smiles that made me reflect on my childhood. Although I grew up in a two-room house—yes, six people in one bedroom—eating lye hominy, not realizing at the time it was a food for poor people, there was so much love, laughter, and food.

Self-Sufficient

I enjoy being self-sufficient, even to the point of going to church and any doctor's appointments alone, without being a burden to anyone. I call Paratransit, a transportation service in the Greater Cleveland area that is part of the Regional Transit Area (RTA); it is for those who are unable to travel on the public-transit system. A one-way trip cost $1.75 from my driveway to the church, doctor's appointment, or any destination I request. I use Paratransit to take me to the community senior-citizens' holiday parties or to the celebrations of family and friends when my children are not available.

Although I am no longer able to visit the sick or those in nursing homes, God gave me a ministry to write letters and send cards to encourage or celebrate birthdays. I have my children, in-laws, over forty grandchildren, nieces, nephews, cousins, and friends whom I mail a birthday card with a few words of encouragement. I am not able to talk on the phone as I used to because of my COPD and its related breathing issues. Excessive talking and other ailments take my breath away, so even a "Thinking of You" card is mailed by me. If I receive a gift from someone, I have one of the children purchase me stamps and a card for a proper thank-you. Sadie, my oldest daughter alive, provides these items generously because she knows I enjoy reaching out to people in this manner.

Initially, my daughter across the street would take me shopping or go for me, depending on my health. This consists of visits to Walgreens for my prescriptions, Aldi for their discount prices on groceries, Marc's for beauty items and soda pops on sale, then Sam's for my cases of Deer Park water, bulk meats, and frozen vegetables. My major shopping was once a month, but gradually my other children and some of my play-adopted children started calling while they were out shopping if they saw things I might want, such as dairy items or fruit.

One time, my children came over as a team and all pitched in to clean, but that was their first and last time. My daughter suggested that I sign up for home health care that would allow cleaners to come in and do my laundry, vacuum, scrub the bathroom, and change my bed linen. Initially, I was not excited or looking forward to anyone coming in my home, but I begrudgingly allowed them to clean. I discovered that the rule was to clean for an hour and talk with me for an hour. I was not lonely and not fond of talking that early in the morning. I preferred the two hours be utilized for quality cleaning. I would get frustrated with some who did not show the best work ethic, staying on the phone or texting.

Lord, is this bigger than a clean house? Do have I to be a light? Am I the only church they will see? I shared *Our Daily Bread* devotionals, and to those who wanted to hear godly advice, God used me to provide.

Losing and Gaining Family

Over the years, I have seen tough times, even the death of my son-in-law who was like a son to me. He was there for me anytime I needed him. My daughter Freda would jokingly say, "Tommy, you know she love you more than me. I'm the in-law!" He would visit me at the apartments and in a quiet manner, not saying but a few words, sit and enjoy my company, and I enjoyed his.

Most recently, my daughter-in-law passed away. When I first met Terri, she thought my family was different because we would have crazy fun without any alcohol in sight. We were a loud and fun household. Many of my children's friends gravitated to our home because of the authentic love of Christ that was displayed. She would call and talk with me, and closer to her passing, we talked more frequently. They both appreciated me, as all my in-laws do, because I never took sides or got in the middle of their marriage.

In the year 2014, I had my husband's side of the family over for the Harrison family reunion. Although the fellowship was small, my children and I learned a lot from my nephew, who once lived with Fred. Curtis shared a lot of stories, and the children were on the edge of their seats in awe to hear stories of their dad. They would laugh at some of the personal but humorous stories and exclaim, "Not my dad!"

Curtis got a chuckle from their pure excitement and said, "Yes, Uncle Freddie!"

What a blessing to keep a close relationship with Fred's family long after his passing.

The same year for Thanksgiving, I flew down to Atlanta, Georgia, to visit my grandson. He met the woman of his dreams and wanted his parents to meet her. Lori and I flew down and had the best time. Her family reminded me of the way my children were back in the day, full of life and laughter. They were down-to-earth, and they appreciated our being real and down-to-earth as well. Lionel was a single parent at the time and was living in a beautiful bi-level home. He had his cousin living on the lower level. I was so proud to see these two young men being responsible and taking care of their daughters.

Doing Life Together

Over the years, the children honored the female elders in the family. They called us the Women of Wisdom (W.O.W.) and gave us sweaters and cardigans with W.O.W. stitched on the fabric on the right side above the chest area. We were treated to a mini concert by the violinist Obie Shelton as he played during our luncheon at the Cheesecake Factory and Zanzibar Soul Fusion restaurant.

Yes, after we older women were forthright about our menu preferences, the W.O.W. events were moved to an upscale, Black-owned restaurant that had soul food. By then, the elderly men were honored as well. Many have transitioned from Earth to heaven, so the W.O.W. events have ended.

The children began going door-to-door, providing lunch or dinner with a treat to each elder's home. No live music, but one-on-one fellowship. I enjoy it because they allow me to help prepare the meals sometimes.

Women of Esther was another group with which I was involved. Most of the women were younger than I, but they showed so much love. They allowed me to speak about my life experiences. This was a Bible-study life group conducted on Sundays at my church. Life groups were designed for members to grow in the Word together, iron sharpening iron, building relationships as well. And that I did. Many of them, to this day, connect with me, even though I have not been able to attend since around 2017. In May, we did our last meeting at Maggiano's, an Italian restaurant. We all wore our tiaras to signify Queen Esther. We had a blast.

One year, cancer seemed to attack many family members and friends. My nephew Jesse called and told me he was battling the disease. I undoubtedly believed he was going to get through this tough challenge. He was one of the most physically fit of the family. He went to the gym regularly, and although he loved food, he kept his weight to a nice size.

His sisters began to call regularly with updates as things became more unsettling. We decided to have monthly family-prayer meetings. We alternated homes for these gatherings. We were asking God to do, as HIS Word says, "exceedingly, abundantly beyond what we could ask or think." We wanted Jesse healed. As the family was drawing closer together, seemingly Jesse's health was getting worse. God decided to answer our prayers for healing Jesse, but not on this side.

We were devastated! Jesse gone? Lord, you took the one who was the first of the extended family to attend college and receive a degree. Everyone admired him for his desire to soar. His wife was beautiful and his daughter so precious. Lord, why the devastation on this ideal family? So many questions.

God may never give us the answer, but we will understand it better, by and by. Maybe it was God's way to bring the family closer and to continue the monthly prayer meetings. Family gatherings were far from those of the days living on Pasadena and in previous homes. Sunday fellowship, heavy-weight-boxing-match parties while watching Mike Tyson, and constant company have been discontinued, but we still celebrate my birthday and have our annual Christmas brunch in my home the Sunday after Christmas.

I laugh when my children check in on me, and I tell them, "It takes a lot for me to do nothing!" At eighty-six, I find so much pleasure in my rituals, which include tuning into Moody Bible Radio, listening to J. D. Greear, watching Trinity

Broadcasting Network's *The Potter's Touch*, *Ron Carpenter*, and *Better Together*, and on Saturdays Charles Stanley. Also, I read the Bible, cover to cover, every year.

This chapter speaks a lot in past tense. Many things were halted, and you will see why in the next chapter.

CHAPTER 17

Plagues

Well, "out with the old, in with the new" is the common New Year's Eve phrase that is quoted when the ball drops. Every year many of us make these New Year's resolutions that are forgotten by February, yet still we look forward to a brand-new year to hit the reset button mentally. We ask ourselves, "How can I be a better me," whether it is to lose weight, eat healthier, save more money, or grow spiritually. We look in our imaginary mirrors, and sometimes a real mirror, to tell ourselves what we will do differently in the upcoming year and what we look forward to that is all positive; it can be as undecorated as simply having peace and good health.

Well, the ball dropped and welcomed 2020. The year was off to a great start. The first Sunday in January, my children and grandchildren surprised me with the annual brunch by allowing me to sit and be served. I had sent letters out before Christmas, telling everyone that I was not up to the cooking. My granddaughter Tamara decided to be the chef. She brought her own style to the kitchen. We thoroughly enjoyed the food and one another. Although, I enjoy having a house full of family and friends, I was appreciative of having only my children and grandchildren. Watching them play family games, as we did in old times, was hilarious.

Sadie brought Pop-O-Matic Trouble, which is my favorite family board game; the players compete to be the first to send all four of their game pieces around the board by the roll of a dice. As I watched Sadie, Ted, Freda, and Lori, who all are well over fifty, stand around me at my dining room table, it brought back memories as they knocked their siblings' game piece out of a slot, sending it back to home base to start all over. Ted was looking like the winner, but then Lori was taking the lead because the girls ganged up on Ted, knocking him out of position. As the laughs and friendly taunts filled the room, Freda out of nowhere came from last place, took the lead, and won the game. A simple lesson to us all—run your own race, no matter how far behind you feel or how bad it looks around you. We all remembered fondly the days of yore playing this game.

This simple family game, Trouble, is what life is full of; there are many steps in the journey to reach our destiny. Life is full of many stumbles as we get knocked off the path. And it is full of many stops that teaches us to not give up, but to simply start over sometimes, creating a new path to arrive at the destination that God had already planned for each of us.

Family Love

The Harrison family's love was what so many admired, but Satan had tried to steal it and destroy the family bond over the years after the death of my youngest son. But, little by little, I see God restoring us. Yes, God promised me in his Scripture, Jeremiah 31: 16–17:

> This is what the LORD says: "Restrain your voice from weeping and your eyes from tears, for your work will be rewarded," declares the LORD. "They will return from the land of the enemy. So there is hope for your future," declares the LORD. "Your children will return to their own land."

God is showing me the fruits of my labor, and my prayers over the many years are being answered. I am not the perfect mom, but I give one hundred percent trying to be the best mom that I know how to be. Everyone's one hundred percent is different, so ask God for wisdom to ultimately be a godly parent because when it is all said and done, it is God we have to give an accounting to. I am blessed to have all my children call me every day or every other day and make sure my needs are met, such as running errands for groceries and other things.

Losing Kobe

The cold months were too harsh for me to go outside. The last time I attended church was the first Sunday in October of 2019 when Paratransit picked me up at my door. I recall feeling sick because the driver went all around Cleveland that Sunday because he had a lot of people to pick up. The long bumpety-bump ride that seemingly hit every bone in my body had me feeling achy and sick all that week.

After that miserable experience, I stayed in the house during the winter months because of all my health issues, plus I wanted to protect myself from the germs of others. I am usually admitted to the hospital two to three times a year because of my breathing issues, but I was determined this year, with God's grace, not to be admitted. Because of people's sniffling, coughing, and spreading germs with their colds, I realized that it was best for me to self-quarantine myself during the winter flu and cold season. I welcomed visitors in my home, but I limited going out unless it was for doctor's appointments.

Sunday, January 26, 2020, I was listening to Sunday sermons from various radio and television pastors, which is my normal Sunday ritual for my spiritual food. Suddenly, there was breaking news in the middle of the afternoon that Kobe Bryant and four other passengers were killed in a helicopter crash. As the news was developing in this competitive business, especially with social media becoming a national unofficial place of mourning, many media outlets were trying to be the first to report with accuracy. Unfortunately, TMZ was the first that accurately announced the death of Kobe that shocked the world. As a fan of basketball, I thoroughly enjoyed watching Kobe Bryant, Shaquille O'Neal, Dwayne Wade, and LeBron James. I cheered for them all because they appeared to be great men, not just on the court, but off the court as well. The only time I did not cheer for them was when they were playing against the Cleveland Cavs. Kobe dead at forty-one! My heart ached for his family.

As the breaking story was developing, the information was becoming inaccurate; there were rumors that all four of his children were in the helicopter. Also, rumor said that Rick Fox was on the helicopter. As time passed and accuracy was restored, I learned his daughter Gianna was on the helicopter. The narrative continued to unfold, announcing his friend, his friend's daughter and wife, and the pilot all died in the crash because of heavy fog. Also, three other friends. There were possibly five families grieving, not to mention the many fans all over the world who loved Kobe as I did. As I watched the various interviews of so many grown men, like Coach Doc Rivers, Shaquille O'Neal, and many athletes, who openly expressed their sadness over the loss of Kobe, my emotions ran deep at seeing those big, strong men cry. I wanted to give them all a hug.

The world mourned for this basketball player phenomenon who was remembered as Black Mamba, Girl Dad, and simply Kobe. All the television networks interviewed those who loved him; many were competitors on the court, but they had high regards for Kobe's competitive, professional athleticism.

A Virus Called COVID-19

I went to my pulmonary doctor near the end of January for my normal checkup. He called me shortly after my visit and suggested that I stay in the house because of a virus called COVID-19. Although there were not many cases reported in Ohio at that time, the doctor considered me at high risk due to my age, breathing issues, and other preexisting conditions, such as a weakened immune system. I did not have a problem with his instructions; his personally calling me made me take this virus seriously.

I figured this quarantine would be over in two weeks, but the virus was becoming aggressive, hitting many states in high numbers until, finally, it was declared a pandemic.

COVID-19 was getting out of control and was spreading all over the world. This infectious disease, which supposedly started in China, is a highly contagious respiratory disease caused by SARS; it is easily spread by droplets released when an infected person coughs, sneezes, or talks. I watched the special reports of Ohio's Governor DeWine report the cases and the deaths.

I decided to cancel my cleaning service. I no longer allowed any of my children or anyone in my home. The personal call from my doctor put a little fear in me. I could not pull away from the television; I kept seeing the reports on the evening news and political channels of many people becoming infected and hospitals bursting at the seams with COVID-19 cases. As the hospitals reached overcapacity, there were refrigerated trucks in the hospital parking lots for the body bags of deceased COVID-19 patients. Funeral homes could not keep up with the demand. This was unbelievable—2020 and there are no quick fixes to take away this major catastrophe!

Governors from many states declared lockdowns and requested, if you had to go out, that you practice social distancing—standing six feet away from anyone else—and wear masks at all times. We were also instructed to wash our hands frequently for at least twenty seconds at a time. Many employers issued laptops for their employees to work remotely until further notice. Employees scrambled to assemble all the necessary tools and items from their desks at work so they could work from home indefinitely.

The pandemic that shut down the world came with subtle stresses and anxiety that raised many questions—such as, how do you get COVID-19? is COVID-19 airborne? and how soon will the Center for Disease Control (CDC) come up with a cure for COVID-19? This was all new to everyone, including professional scientists.

As we entered spring, COVID-19 cases were increasing all over the world. I watched the corona numbers in Ohio for those hospitalized and those who died. New cases were reported daily. Governor DeWine gave a briefing daily that I watched faithfully.

My daughter went shopping for my bulk items at Sam's, only to see the store shelves empty of Lysol disinfectant spray, paper towels, and toilet tissue. Initially, she was extremely uncomfortable being in public places, so she was trying to decide if shopping as soon as the stores opened to ensure the items were not sold out was the best time to shop, versus at the end of the day when there were fewer people. Decisions! Decisions!

Initially, the Lord was protecting my family from COVID-19, but then we thought it hit us. Sunday, April 12, I received a call that my first great-grandson, Man-Man, passed in Michigan, and I could not be there to hug my eldest grandson, Richard. I buried three children, so although I did not know his personal pain, I knew the general pain of losing a child. We assumed the cause of death was COVID-19 because he was healthy and vibrant.

Here I am, feeling a heavy heart. Did I hurt for me? Momentarily! But the hurt immediately flew to the parents and siblings. Your heart aches so bad for them. This is the son of my oldest daughter, Gwen, who died. Whose shoulder will Richard cry on? Who will be there to comfort him during this time when he feels the need to be strong for everyone else?

Watching Man-Man's Celebration of Life service on Facebook was painful. If I'd had a bucket of fried chicken, I would have consumed the entire thing. Satan uses pain to try to tempt you to do something that will provide momentary satisfaction, but that is not good for you. I thank God I had no temptations in my home, such as chicken, cake, cookies, or any comfort foods. I was scattered emotionally all over the place, wanting to do something to ease the pain of my family in Michigan.

COVID-19 robbed me and others of the type of closure that we are accustomed to when we funeralize loved ones. Closure for me is hugging your loved ones and being there for those hurting the most. The blessing in the pain is that Man-Man had recently visited me in Cleveland before COVID-19. Although I did not get the current pictures of his family that he was going to mail me, I saw him in person and got a hug. As time passed, the autopsy results were revealed. Man-Man passed from natural causes, not COVID-19.

Shortly after the death of my great-grandson, my first cousin, his wife, and his daughter were diagnosed with coronavirus. Jesus! My cousin is high risk; he is close to my age and uses an oxygen tank. Things were not looking good! His children, nieces, nephews, and distant family members who were on Facebook came together virtually to pray every Saturday. God, who is sovereign, allowed my cousin to transition from this life to eternity. God answered our prayers of healing. He healed two of them, his wife and daughter, on this side, but my cousin Roosevelt was healed on the other side with a glorious body. Another funeral service I was unable to attend, leaning not on my own understanding, but trusting God with all my heart in this rough coronavirus season.

Well, the end of spring was drawing near. My daughter went flower shopping for me. Our annual tradition of planting flowers to make the front yard and backyard look nice would be necessary this year as an extra boost to see something positive with these eyes. She had her pots in the driveway, and I sat on the porch with mine. When I finished planting a pot, she, mask on, took the beautifully planted pot from me and gave me a new one. We worked through the day until every pot was filled with a colorful arrangement of flowers. After she placed every pot in its spot, she poured the red mulch around the pots for the yard to be filled with beauty. I enjoyed looking out my window to see the lovely arrangement of flowers.

May 30, my grandson drove from Georgia with his beautiful wife to pick up his daughter for summer break. They stood in the driveway, chitchatting with me for a little while before doing a quick turnaround and getting back on the freeway to Georgia to return at a decent time. I was so happy to see them. As they were about to leave, I noticed my daughter decorating the yard with paper flowers and balloons.

Later, I saw a procession of cars; the people in the cars were blowing their horns and waving as they drove by my house. They circled and came back around to wish me a happy birthday. My children and grandchildren provided chocolate-covered strawberries and balloons to all the participants. They jumped out of their cars and spoke into the microphone that was placed on the edge of the lawn near the public sidewalk; sanitizer and disinfectant wipes were even provided for everyone. My children had used every safety measure.

The love from family and friends was special. After being in isolation for many months and watching my grandson's funeral on Facebook, I appreciated the people coming around with a smile and soothing words, big birthday signs, cards, and gifts of love. What an amazing birthday celebration for me! I did not have to cook or prepare for folks to come. I just sat in my rocking chair on the porch and received the love as I smiled, blew kisses, and gave big air hugs.

The Chief Medical Advisor to the President, Dr. Fauci, and Director of the Ohio Department of Health, Dr. Acton, were all concerned about the various summer-holiday gatherings; they pleaded with us to avoid holiday gatherings in order to avoid a spike in COVID-19 cases. Medical staff all over the world were exhausted, and they were concerned that a spike would cause weariness in the hospitals among the workers.

My sister called me on a Saturday after her birthday, which was in late June. Our conversation was so fruitful and long. We talked for over an hour. I was reminded of her visit with me before COVID-19. Her husband had a doctor's appointment, so her daughter Norma dropped her off to spend time with me while she took her dad to his appointment. Although I believe my sister had dementia—because of previous conversations in which she seemed to be reliving her younger years and couldn't remember a close family member—nevertheless, everything she said made sense to me. Maybe because I was glad she was with me. I wanted her to be with me; we were not getting any younger.

The last birthday she celebrated was her ninety-first. She told her daughter, "I want a yard birthday party just as my sister has all the time." Her children granted her a social-distancing birthday party in the yard.

Shortly after, she was diagnosed with health issues and was admitted in the hospital. While in the hospital, she tested positive for COVID-19. We prayed for a healing! The nurse called the family to set up a Zoom call to give their good-byes because things did not look hopeful, according to the nurse. I was so concerned for her husband of over seventy-plus years and her children.

Lord, if this is the end of this earthly chapter for my sister, then I prefer to cherish the memory of her sitting at my dining room table and having a meal with me or sitting on my couch reminiscing. I forfeited the Zoom call.

Three days after they did their Zoom call, I was notified that my sister passed. I must remind myself that if the Bible speaks of Job worshipping after hearing the news of his seven dead children, why can't I worship after hearing about the loss of a loved one. I know God's Word says, "We know all things work together for good!" I accept the death, but the pain is real.

During this COVID-19 season, I learned to pray and trust God more. Only God can stop this virus. It gives me confidence that whatever happens is His will. God has an end date for all of us.

Again, we prayed for healing, and God answered our prayers—maybe not our way, but His. As mentioned, God heals in two ways. He heals them and brings them back to us, or heals them and calls them to Him. We must understand that when we pray for God's healing, He has the last say on how He heals.

Racial-Tension Flashback

Watching the stories unfold about Ahmaud Arbery, George Floyd, Breonna Taylor had me regurgitating the hate by Whites that many of my loved ones experienced in the South. If you are unaware of these three individuals, allow me to briefly recap their tragic deaths.

In February 2020, Arbery, a young Black man jogging down the road, was chased by three White male residents near Brunswick, Georgia. He was shot three times and accused of burglary, according to Travis McMichaels, who, investigators said, used racial epithets after he shot Arbery and stood over his body. McMichaels's father was in his pickup truck with a friend and videotaped the incident. The video footage was made public in May 2020 and went viral. Thank God for slowing life down for many to see this clear act of racism. Many people protested for justice.

March 2020, Breonna Taylor was fatally shot six times when thirty-two bullets were fired after three White police officers dressed in plain clothes forced entry into her apartment. According to Taylor's boyfriend, Kenneth Walker, the police officers did not knock, announce themselves, or issue a warning. Walker thought the officers were intruders and fired a warning shot that struck an officer in the leg. None of the officers were indicted, which provoked civil unrest and continued protests across the country. Allegedly, the officers said they had a "no-knock" search warrant due to suspicion of drug trafficking that had been confirmed by the postal service investigator. The postal investigator stated that no such collaboration between the police and postal service ever occurred.

May 2020, White officer Derek Chauvin, with his knee to Floyd's neck, pinned George Floyd to the ground for what many believed to be eight minutes and forty-six seconds. Two store employees believed Floyd paid for his cigarettes with a counterfeit twenty-dollar bill, so they called the police. Shortly after, Floyd was handcuffed and was being taken across the street to be placed in a police car; a bystander began videoing the encounter that went viral. Floyd was shown on the ground next to the police car, repeatedly saying he couldn't breathe and later crying for his mama moments before dying. People all over the world were disturbed by this video footage of police brutality and systemic racism. This incident of seeing someone executed right before many of our eyes evoked rage.

The country was already stressed by the COVID-19 pandemic. So, seeing these acts of blatant racial injustice sparked protest after protest all over the world. This prompted dialogues between White churches and Black churches, uniting them for the common cause of justice and peace. These racial injustices opened the eyes of many Whites and forced them to recognize their blind spots of White privilege. Many Whites openly admitted that they finally understood why Blacks were uncomfortable being pulled over by police officers. Many began to understand why Black men, fathers and sons, talk about how to act if pulled over by a police officer. Story after story of police brutality and racism were hitting the media screens.

Later, the "Karen" stories began circulating. Karens are caricatures of White, racist, middle-aged women who act entitled and demand their way beyond what's normal or reasonable. One example happened Memorial Day 2020. Christian Cooper, a blackbird watcher, was walking in Central Park when he ran into a White woman—Amy Cooper, no relation. She had her dog off the lead. He asked her to put her dog back on the lead since the area was leash-only. She called 911, flipping the story and saying, "There's an African American man threatening my life."

Christian filmed the entire incident because his life could have been at risk with the police, but thank God no harm was brought to him. Also, because of her false report, her employer put her on administrative leave, and she was forced to surrender the dog, which was a rescue animal, back to the rescue organization after they saw the video of how she was handling the dog.

These 2020 racist incidents struck to my core. I was reminded of an incident in which a young man was walking home from work. A White man had his father's truck, ran him off the road, and killed him just because of the color of his rich-in-melanin skin.

Another story imprinted in my mind from the South and regurgitated because of the current injustice was when a White man did not pay a Black young man his earnest wages for his labor. The Black young man took it upon himself to take one of the man's chickens. He took it home, his Mother cooked it, and when they were all sitting down at the table for dinner, the White man came to their home, took the man outside, and hung him in front of his parents' home.

Another incident that I remember was going to the store, and when I finished getting what I needed, I walked to the cashier to pay. Just then, a White person stepped into the store, so I had to step aside and wait until after the White person finished shopping, paid for their purchases, and left the store, before the cashier would ring my purchase.

Also, after cleaning a White person's entire home, I had to exit out the back door.

The racist White man is fervently saying, "Ain't no one like me; we are top dog; we are superior!"

Racial and political tensions seemingly heightened in 2020 and really showed me that although I knew racism still existed, this challenging year revealed that many are becoming independent from God, and the consequences of our sins are being materialized. Thank God for laws and legislation that have made some major changes for equality. Although, there is so much more work to be done. We can use the philosophy of Congressman John Lewis who says, "When you see something that is not right, not fair, not just, say something! Do something! Get in trouble! Good trouble! Necessary trouble!"

As I read through the Tony Evans New Study Bible this year and thoroughly enjoyed his commentary, God was leading me to read the Recovery Study Bible in 2021. We must meditate on the Word of God and protect our peace. COVID-19 may have me in quarantine, but I am able to listen to the Word from great television evangelists or radio pastors, such as Charles Stanley, T. D. Jakes, J. D. Greear, Ron Carpenter, and Tony Evans. On good days when I can figure out my phone, I retrieve the sermons from my pastor, Kevin James. Also, I call the Heal Our Land prayer line that my daughter and grandson facilitate with various prayer warriors. Staying connected with the Body of Christ and other Christian believers encourages me to keep pushing.

Life is a bowl of cherries full of pits! Some people can look all shiny on the outside, but there is pain that may cause a war on the inside. Regurgitating pain could cause me to be bitter and angry, but I choose to stay in the Word and let it go, surrendering all to Christ. Think of it as having ten dollars at the start of the day. After a full day, you go to get the ten dollars, but cannot find it. It is lost. You backtrack to every place you have been, but still cannot find it. You can allow it to be a robber and destroy your joy and peace. Or you can simply let it go, move forward, and work hard to earn another ten dollars.

Life is about choices. What do you choose? I choose the fruits of the spirit: peace, love, joy, goodness, gentleness, patience, kindness, faithfulness, and self-control. God can grant you the peace and strength to endure every step, stumble, and stop.

My song this year, as I enter 2021, is "Just a Closer Walk with Thee."

I am weak but Thou art strong
Jesus keep me from all wrong
I'll be satisfied as long
As I walk, let me walk close to Thee

Just a closer walk with Thee
Grant it, Jesus, is my plea
Daily walking close to Thee
Let it be, dear Lord, let it be

When my feeble life is o'er
Time for me will be no more
Guide me gently, safely o'er
To Thy kingdom's shore, to Thy shore

Just a closer walk with Thee
Grant it, Jesus, is my plea
Daily walking close to Thee
Let it be, dear Lord, let it be

CHAPTER 18

Healthy: Physically, Financially, Spiritually, Emotionally, and Mentally

Prayer and Fasting

I thought this book was finished, but I must share my journey of early 2022—the beginning of a New Year of praying, fasting, and praying that God will heal our land from all the variants of COVID-19 and that God will heal me and make me completely healthy spiritually, physically, emotionally, mentally, and financially. Yes, I'm a firm believer in the power of prayer and fasting. Mark 9:29 of the King James Version says, "This kind can *come* forth by nothing, but *by prayer and fasting."*

January 1, 2022, let the fast begin by eliminating meat and salt from my diet. I LOVE salt! I cook with salt and then use the saltshaker for additional seasoning once I sit at the dining room table with my plate. I have always overseasoned my food. During my childhood, I took a biscuit, opened it up, doused one side with hot sauce until it was red, then shook salt on it until it turned white. I seasoned my meats with hot sauce, salt, paprika, and Watkins black pepper. I'm sure you've heard the lie we believe—"Now, that's good eating!" This is a new season and a new day. Old bad habits stop here, by God's grace. Let the being healthy physically begin with NO MORE SALT!

Yes, I'm a firm believer in the power of prayer and fasting. Matthew 17:21 says, "Howbeit this kind goeth not out but by prayer and fasting." I started fasting as a little girl with my mom. We would fast every Tuesday and Friday until noon. We used the entire Psalms 119 that was passed down from my grandmother as one of the greatest Scriptures. I memorized all 176 verses. We fasted more as a ritual or to show God that we were giving up food, but our empty stomachs didn't line up with our hearts.

I recall, on those fasting days, how my mom would cook a big breakfast for the family. She and I would make our plates and save them for later. One day, I placed my plate on top of the stove, only to come in the kitchen to see the cat on the stove enjoying my food. I was so upset that I stuffed him in the oven and shut the door.

I forgot all about the cat, but God brought it back to my remembrance. I opened the oven door; the cat jumped out, ran out the door, and was never seen again. No, not a godly fast.

Now, I'm grown and living in the big city—Cleveland, Ohio—with a husband, children, and bills. Here I am, abstaining from food but again my attitude was off-the-chain ugly! I was irritable all the time.

The Lord spoke in my spirit, "Mae, I'd rather you have a full stomach and pure heart than an empty stomach and an evil heart."

So I stopped fasting for a long time. I continued to read my Bible and spend a lot of time listening to Moody Bible Radio on WCRF and watching Christian television, such as TCT,

TBN, and Daystar. I continued serving people, my church, and my family.

Healthy Physically

One day, Lori introduced me to The 40-Day Sugar Fast: Where Physical Detox Meets Spiritual Transformation by Wendy Speake. I read the book and gave up sugar, coffee, meat, and bread. The Lord delivered me completely from sugar and coffee in February 2020.

Also, God delivered me from diet soda pops. I use to drink two per day, but I surrendered it to the Lord. I planned my 2022 goals on December 18, 2021. I wanted to be faithful to the Lord so that I could lay aside this physical weight. I remember being 321 pounds two weeks after losing my youngest son, Freddie, in August 1990. I'm currently 213.2 pounds. Praise God from Whom all blessings flow!

Reaching into my past again, I grew up poor, so a roof over our heads and plenty to eat were my parents' main goals. Dad worked hard for $6.25 per week. Mom went to the commodity house once a month, where they would distribute rations to the poor. You were given a coupon book that allowed you to get sugar, flour, and white butter with a coloring you mixed in it to make it yellow. As mentioned in earlier chapters, later we owned vegetable and fruit gardens, chickens, hogs, cows, goats, pear and peach orchards, to name a few. Food was plentiful, and I ate until my stomach ached. Yes, I was indeed full.

Today, I'm thankful that food no longer has a stronghold on me. Although I'm a work in progress, I'm glad I'm not where I used to be. I'm asking God to allow me to see 185 pounds on this side. My breathing is better because of my clean eating. My diabetes and blood pressure are under control. I no longer take high-blood-pressure pills or diabetes medicine because of the change in my diet.

Healthy Financially

Dear Lord, I give my finances unto you! Deliver me from wasteful spending and giving more to others than I have to give. Lord, bring me back to the ten-ten-eighty rule—ten percent tithes, ten percent savings, and eighty percent expenses. Lord, give me a desire to be a good steward to the finances that you entrusted to me. Let everything be done to your glory.

My respect for money has never been high. If I may go back down memory lane, every Saturday, my dad took us to town. He gave each of his children fifty cents. My brothers slipped into the theater for a cowboy movie. My sister went to the Field and Brook to get a ten-cent ice cream cone, but I went to the discount store to purchase a Bible for twenty-five cents, then to the food wagon to purchase hamburgers, two for fifteen cents, with an RC Cola for five cents. I topped it off with a big Butter Nut candy bar for five cents.

Dad, put his foot down after so many visits to town, told me I could not buy any more Bibles, but to enjoy the stack that I'd accumulated. Lord, bless my finances.

Healthy Spiritually

Spiritually, paraphrasing Psalms 42, "I'm as the deer that thirsts for water. So, my soul thirsts for you, Lord, the Living Word." As mentioned, my love for purchasing Bibles is still the same. I don't indulge as often, but I do love the smell of a new leather, big-print Bible. I have two in each room of my house. I've purchased the Recovery Bible, Charles Stanley's,

Tony Evans's, to name a few study Bibles. I have purchased a Bible for every one of my children, grandchildren, great-grandchildren, and some play-adopted children.

Since I was old enough to purchase Bibles, I have also enjoyed reading them. Back in the day, it wasn't cool to tote a Bible, but I carried mine to church to learn and to keep up with the pastor.

One day, the pastor's wife approached me and asked, "Sis Mabel, are you going to be a preacher?"

I replied, "No, ma'am!"

One thing I recall the pastor preaching on a scorching-hot summer day in Mississippi was "Hell is hotter than it is today!" Yes, he was right! According to Matthew 13:42 of the New International Version, "They will throw them into the blazing furnace, where there will be weeping and gnashing of teeth." But Romans 6:23 says, "For the wages of sin is death, but the gift of God is eternal life through Jesus Christ our Lord."

Currently, I have plenty of time to spend with God. I read two devotionals at the top of the morning; in the evening I read the Word of God because I enjoy reading through the Bible from Genesis to Revelations every year. I read many Christian books or encouraging and inspirational books that educate me, such as *Full: Food, Jesus, and the Battle for Satisfaction* by Asheritah Ciuciu.

Healthy Emotionally and Mentally

I'm in a new season of really asking God, "Lord, what will you have me do?" I want to live in God's Will in 2022. My income is more than fifty cents. Currently, I pay beyond ten percent in tithes.

I purchase food and paper goods, such as toilet tissue, Kleenex, and paper towels. I recently figured out the sky won't fall if my inventory is low. If I don't have ten rolls of paper towels, ten pounds of wings, two to four bags of four-pack vegetables, two to twelve pounds of turkey, and four forty-pack cases of water, then so be it. My heart would flutter if I got down to one case of water, but yet I sing, "The Center of My Joy," "I'm ALL in," and other songs that confess my love for God. Clothes and shoes are not at the top of my list; those are Johnny-come-latelies, but something about an overstocked refrigerator and freezer always gave me a sense of security!

My prayer this season is that God will show me my real needs. My responsibility for this season. Lord, Thy kingdom come; Thy will be done, in and through me, starting over again at eighty-seven and a half. Lord, help me emotionally and mentally as I embark on this fast January 1, 2022.

I am trying to face what hurts me. It is still too tender! My best friend, Maggie J., passed away. Her funeral was on Lori's birthday, December 14, 2021. My only living son, Ted, attended her Homegoing service. I was able to stream it. I saw my son going around and hugging people he hadn't seen in a long time.

After the service, he called me as he was walking to his vehicle to leave. "Hey, Mom, I saw from a distance Bro Ray, Bro Yarbrough—"

I stopped him and said, "Bro S. Yarbrough lives out of state; it was probably his brother."

He laughed. "Yeah, yeah!"

He sounded so joyful and happy to me, even on such a tough day and occasion. He saw so many old friends at Good Shepherd. What was a sad time brought a little joy for him from reuniting with old friends. As he was leaving the church, he climbed in his vehicle and was bragging and reminiscing about his "baby girl's" baby shower that I was unable to attend due to being high risk during another surge of the virus. He shared how he was able to sing "The Center of My Joy" to the unborn baby at the shower. He also told me about playing with his son's baby boy, Judah, who was thirteen months old at the time. He was proud to be able to put Baby Judah to sleep.

On Christmas Eve, ten days later, I received the call that Ted was admitted to the hospital. He was unresponsive when the EMT workers got to him. The doctor said it looked grim, and there was nothing that they could do because he'd been unconscious for forty-five minutes. Later, I got the call that he passed due to COVID and blood clots in his lung and heart.

Ted had decided to stop taking his blood thinners, and he refused to get the vaccine. As a mother, I constantly worried about his being high risk; he was overweight and had other health concerns. We had conversations about the vaccine, but I could not convince him. I told him that my doctor called and said I couldn't be around anyone who didn't have the vaccine because I was high risk. I asked him to pray about reconsidering getting the vaccine.

From my perspective, my son chose to play Russian roulette with God. Guess who is going to win that game? Ted's death hit me like a ton of bricks; I had just seen him being so social and full of life and vigor! God knew my son's end date. Ted told me his income was ending in February, and he didn't know what was going to happen, BUT GOD DID.

Lord, strengthen me emotionally and mentally during this challenging time of seeing my fourth child gone too soon. God spoke in my spirit, "'For my thoughts are not your thoughts, neither are your ways my ways,' declared the LORD. 'As the heavens are higher than the earth, so are my ways higher than your ways and my thoughts than your thoughts'" (Isaiah 55:8–9).

God allowed a tree to spruce up with three leaves in my hens-and-chicks planter the day after Ted passed. It was as if God was speaking to me through a random tree; he was telling me to focus on my three blessings who are alive—Sadie, Freda, and Lori—and not the pain of my past.

God spoke again with my landline, oddly. The word *PEACE* appeared on my display, instead of the usual date and time. I believe God speaks to His children in so many personal ways to comfort the hurting and to provide that peace that surpasses all understanding.

Although there were challenging seasons in my life, I'm sure there will be more. God's Word says, "In this world you will have tribulations, but be of good cheer. I have overcome the world" (John 16:33, New King James Version). I'd rather go through the difficult times with Jesus, than attempt to go through all these challenges without Him. He has strengthened me through ever step, stumble, and stop.

True Fasting

Shout it aloud, do not hold back.

Raise your voice like a trumpet.

Declare to my people their rebellion

and to the descendants of Jacob their sins.

For day after day they seek me out;

they seem eager to know my ways,

as if they were a nation that does what is right

and has not forsaken the commands of its God.

They ask me for just decisions

and seem eager for God to come near them.

'Why have we fasted,' they say,

'and you have not seen it?

Why have we humbled ourselves,

and you have not noticed?'

Yet on the day of your fasting, you do as you please

and exploit all your workers.

Your fasting ends in quarreling and strife,

and in striking each other with wicked fists.

You cannot fast as you do today

and expect your voice to be heard on high.

Is this the kind of fast I have chosen,

only a day for people to humble themselves?

Is it only for bowing one's head like a reed

and for lying in sackcloth and ashes?
Is that what you call a fast,
a day acceptable to the LORD?

Is not this the kind of fasting I have chosen:
to loose the chains of injustice
and untie the cords of the yoke,
to set the oppressed free
and break every yoke?
Is it not to share your food with the hungry
and to provide the poor wanderer with shelter—
when you see the naked, to clothe them,
and not to turn away from your own flesh and blood?
Then your light will break forth like the dawn,
and your healing will quickly appear;
then your righteousness will go before you,
and the glory of the LORD will be your rear guard.
Then you will call, and the LORD will answer;
you will cry for help, and he will say: Here am I.

If you do away with the yoke of oppression,
with the pointing finger and malicious talk,
and if you spend yourselves in behalf of the hungry
and satisfy the needs of the oppressed,
then your light will rise in the darkness,
and your night will become like the noonday.
The LORD will guide you always;

he will satisfy your needs in a sun-scorched land
and will strengthen your frame.
You will be like a well-watered garden,
like a spring whose waters never fail.
Your people will rebuild the ancient ruins
and will raise up the age-old foundations;
you will be called Repairer of Broken Walls,
Restorer of Streets with Dwellings.

If you keep your feet from breaking the Sabbath
and from doing as you please on my holy day,
if you call the Sabbath a delight
and the LORD's holy day honorable,
and if you honor it by not going your own way
and not doing as you please or speaking idle words,
then you will find your joy in the LORD,
and I will cause you to ride in triumph on the heights of the land
and to feast on the inheritance of your father Jacob.
For the mouth of the LORD has spoken.
(Isaiah 58, New International Version)

25 Things about Mae Bell Harrison

1. I love my family, including my many play-adopted children.

2. I'm an extrovert—I love people.

3. I read my Bible front to back every year.

4. I call out every child and grandchild by name in my daily prayers.

5. I'm a leader—my nickname is Sergeant.

6. I'm known as the woman who smiles in good times and bad.

7. I never meet a stranger.

8. My philosophy: If there are no leftovers when you cook, then somebody didn't get full.

9. I live by: What's in your hand? USE IT!

10. I LOVE a good church hat.

11. I love to cook.

12. I don't like mushrooms.

13. NBA basketball is my favorite sport—I write letters to Shaq, and he responds.

14. My favorite holiday is Thanksgiving.

15. I love the dirt; planting flowers and gardening are my therapy.

16. I journal and log my vitals every day—weight, blood pressure, and sugar count.

17. I never use an alarm clock. Jesus is my alarm clock for early morning appointments.

18. I don't like escalators.

19. I don't like the sight of snakes, even if just on television.

20. I don't turn my television on until after 5:00 p.m.

21. My favorite color is mint green.

22. I only drink Deer Park bottled water.

23. I usually listen to my seasoned television/radio pastors, but I listen to Michael Todd too.

24. I've been single and satisfied since I became a widow at the age of fifty-one.

25. I only write in cursive; rarely do I print.

Memorable Moments in My Home!

Scenario 1

My dad always led prayers on Sunday morning, saying the following: "Dear Lord, bless us with what we need, and drive our wants away."

In my mind, I'm saying, *What?*

After a few Sundays passed, and I kept hearing this prayer, I told my siblings, "Y'all, we ain't going to have nothing!"

They asked, "Why, Mabel?"

I said, "Did you hear Daddy's prayer? He said, 'Bless us with what we need, and drive our wants away.'"

My siblings laughed uncontrollably and said, "Mabel, you a fool."

Scenario 2

My mom gave my siblings and me the work-ethic speech: "This house rolls on six wheels—Dad, Mom, and four children. If one of you is slacking off, it leaves his or her load on the rest of us. Be sure to pull your own load."

Scenario 3

Robert was our oldest brother. He was in charge when our parents were not home. At breakfast, he fried four pork steaks and made rice with gravy.

I was a fast, greedy eater. Fannie and Mozel ate slowly. I knew they had weak stomachs, so I got the castor oil and turned the bottle up so it would drip into my mouth. They were so grossed out that they ran out the back door, leaving their meat, and I ate it!

I got away with doing that many times, but one day Robert caught me because they'd run to the back door and yelled. Robert whipped me good. After that incident, I stopped pulling pranks.

I've hated castor oil since that day.

Scenario 4

My siblings and I went to the store with five cents each. Robert got a Butter Nut.

I begged Robert for some of his candy bar.

He said, "If God will keep the scent out of your nose, then I will keep the taste from your mouth."

Scenario 5

A tornado came through our community and literally picked up our two-room home and turned it around; the front door was now the back door. The storm took the chimney, and the tin roof landed in pieces in the gully and trees.

Prior, Mom had cooked neck bones. As she saw the storm damaging the house, she hollered out, "Get on your bed!"

I reached in the pot and got me a neck bone. While everyone was screaming and crying because the house was damaged from the storm, I was satisfied because I had grabbed me a neck bone.

I was only ten years old, so I thought it was funny when I saw my uncle Luther crying, "I want my mother!" Lawd, I was high on my neck bone.

Thank God, none of us was hurt. We all went to town and stayed with my grandma.